AF884849

MONEY
MATTERS
UNIVERSITY

EQUIPPING YOU TO RETAIN WEALTH

MONEY MATTERS UNIVERSITY
EQUIPPING YOU TO RETAIN WEALTH

First Printing 2025
ISBN: 978-1-968772-04-8

www.MoneyMattersUniversity.com

MONEY MATTERS UNIVERSITY

EQUIPPING YOU TO RETAIN WEALTH

Discussion #19

Risk Management

Discussion #19

Risk Management

Discussion #19

Risk Management

The Big Idea:

Taking stock of negative possible outcomes gives us an ability to work to negate them.

1 Understanding Risk

https://youtu.be/g4QHC-KF4FE

Watch video

By my early or mid 40s, I had been practicing accounting for 20+ years. Around that time my neighbor came over one day, and started to tell me what he did for a living. As he talked, I listened, yet my eyes were starting to glaze over. I started to ask myself, "What is this guy talking about?"

But he kept going. As the words kept coming, I realized he was talking about something he called "risk management." But I had no idea what that was, even with all of my work experience.

Within a few years, he taught me so much about risk management. Those lessons have given me tremendous insight into how to run my company and build my own financial habits.

It was a game changer for me.

In a similar way, I desire to teach you about finances and financial literacy—which just happens to include understanding our risk.

Risk often impacts finances.

That guy gave me advice which was very practical and saved me a lot of headache later in life.

Since then, I have come to see that few of us take time to know our possible risks and how to mitigate them. At times, just like I was with my neighbor, I bet others might feel a bit glazed over when I talk. But it is worth it to lean in and make sure that each of us have a strong financial foundation.

My introduction to risk management was confusing at first, but helpful as I learned. Why do I start with this story? Because I want you to know that even though I was in a professional financial industry for 20 years in a senior financial position, I didn't know what risk management was. So if you don't know what it means, don't fret over it. I didn't know what it meant either.

To be prepared for what could come, let's take some time and try to break down exactly what risk management means.

Building Financial Language:

When was the first time you heard about risk management?

____

____

____

____

____

____

2 What Is Risk Management?

https://youtu.be/xzI4At0zjtw

Watch video

Let's start to define what risk management means. Risk management is defined as *managing* risk. Now I know you're not supposed to use the same words in your definition as the term, but we must think about the word manage.

Manage means that you have to oversee something.

You have to watch it. You need to have an understanding of what's happening. Next, you must make decisions.

We take risks every day. We may not see it in our day-to-day, but risks are all around us. We do things that are quite common which incur risks. For example, every time we get in our car, there's a risk. *What's the risk*?

There's a risk of being involved in an accident. There's a risk that we could run out of gas if we don't look and make sure we have enough gas to get us where we are going.

There's some form of risk in many of our actions, but we don't think of it as a risk. We just think of it as our day-to-day living.

But when it comes to risk management in our everyday life, there are certain things we have to watch. In many of these things, we may have little to no control over the outcome if we choose to leave it alone.

But there is another way.

We can take action to protect ourselves, if we dare to look at the risks around us.

Building Financial Language:

At a high level, what daily activities do you see as carrying a risk?

____

____

____

____

How often do you think about strategies to mitigate that risk?

____

____

____

____

3 How To Identify Risk

Watch video

https://youtu.be/pE-GkV557vs

The proper way of managing your risk is to *identify* all of your risks. To have, let's say, a round table with the "powers to be."

If it's a bigger company, this might mean gathering the board of directors, leaders, or business owners.

I have a small practice. This gives me the ability to bring everybody in and have a discussion. I want us to be able to talk about our risks together. There is power in us coming together as a team to define what those risks are. *Our goal*?

We want to understand our potential maximum risk.

As best as we can, we choose to look at that. Then we are able to mitigate that risk or decide to take that risk.

There is something called "self-insure." Some decide they want to self-insure. This means they see a risk factor as being quite low. They see those damages as being so minimal that it's not worth spending any money to mitigate that risk.

That is up to them, they can make that choice.

Each of us gets to choose. *My advice*? It is best to take inventory of what our risks *could* be. Identifying how much that risk could cost in a quantitative manner allows us to then decide whether or not there's a cost benefit to invest in eliminating the risk or reducing it.

Building Financial Language:

Pick one risk that you or your company face. Next, select one way to mitigate it.

____

____

____

____

____

Do you see that risk as being high or low? And why?

____

____

____

4 Personal Risk Management

https://youtu.be/tGv3lEOmvD8

Watch video

Let's talk about risk management from an individual side. I want to start with an auto insurance policy. Every state has their own requirements for auto insurance. When shopping for a policy, the first thing most people do is ask for a quote. Once you give a provider the vehicle's VIN number, they know everything about your car. They know when it was manufactured, if there were any accidents, the weight of the car, and the risk factors of that vehicle—including how safe it is. All of these factors go into how much it costs in order to get a policy.

Once you know what the quote is, if it is too expensive you can either go to another provider or ask them, "What does the policy include?" Find out what the limits are for property, bodily injury, collision, and comprehensive, along with whether it is stacking or non-stacking. Each one of these terms has a reason and a cost, but there are minimums.

When you're on a budget, it's not uncommon to want the lowest level of coverage in order to stay at or above the minimum requirements. In the end, it is your choice if you want to take the risk.

Is it worth only taking the minimum with a brand new car that you just spent $75,000 on? Or would it be worth it to do that with a car that I bought for $1,500 since it is falling apart? These are choices we get to make. But what about medical coverage? What if another driver is injured? What if somebody gets hurt? What if somebody gets killed and they don't have insurance and we get sued?

We have to think through what risk we are willing to take.

Unfortunately, here and there and insurance agents will just want load you down even if it means you are over-insured. Yet many individuals just want to spend the least amount of money and could be under-insured. There has to be balance.

So what am I saying? I'm saying we need to learn. It's really important to figure out what coverage exists. While we have only talked about auto insurance, it is the same thing for medical insurance, homeowner's insurance, contents insurance for renters, and so on. It is important to understand what a policy is protecting.

What is the investment that you're spending?
What is the recovery you could get?

Insurance is simply a tool to manage risk. That's why we each need a really good, honest insurance agent to walk us through the options and help us understand what we need.

Building Financial Language:

What is your relationship like with each of your insurance agents?

____

____

____

____

5 The Risk Management Framework

Watch video

https://youtu.be/5DNwE2bg56w

Let's talk about the framework of risk management. First is avoidance. Avoidance means you don't engage in risky activity. From a personal perspective, you can control your actions and avoid behavior which could cause a negative outcome. For example, if you want to prevent getting cancer from smoking, just don't smoke. However, there are people who get cancer from secondhand smoke, which you may not be able to control.

Next is retention. Retention means you are willing to hold a risk yourself. You are not worried about it. You know exactly what your risk would be and have decided it is worthwhile to maintain that risk.

The third category is to share the risk. A good example of this is a PEO, a People Employment Organization. This is a co-employment agreement in an organization which is used to leverage the cost of medical insurance, lower administrative fees, and file tax returns. The risk is shared together.

Next, we have transfer. Transfer is when you take your risk and give it to a third party. An example of this is mitigating risk by paying for an insurance policy. It doesn't fully eliminate risk since there is often a deductible. In this case, a deductible is your risk.

Another category is defined as loss prevention and reduction. This is when we minimize risk with another activity. A good example of this is offering gym memberships to employees and serving healthy lunches.

These activities minimize the risk.

Somebody who is healthier is less likely to get sick and have as many claims. Therefore, this is a way to minimize the loss ratio so that with fewer claims, the insurance company pays out. The more profitable the insurance company is, the less likely they are to increase rates significantly. I have seen rates go up 60-75% due to employees filing huge claims. This doesn't seem fair. But this is what is known as the census. The census of that employer had very high risk because of the loss ratio, (i.e the cost of claims relative to the cost of the policy).

Because of that history, that insurance company is essentially saying, "We don't want your business. We're happy to raise your rates." This forces you to shop for a new policy. And that's not always easy to do.

Building Financial Language:

As you review your personal life or your company, can you find an example of each type of risk?

Avoidance:____

Retention:____

Shared Risk: ______________________________________

Transfer:____

Prevention And Reduction: ____________________________

6 How To Select Insurance

https://youtu.be/ECVqWjDlVAo

Watch video

How might you select an insurance company? The first key is to understand what your need is and what your plans are. Next, you need to know what your risks could be. My suggestion is to make a list of all of the areas that might have a risk. Then, take a look at an insurance company who is willing to have that risk transfered to them. *Why*? Because the best way of mitigating risk is through some form of insurance.

This is how to determine whether or not you can get a good insurance policy that helps you manage that risk. You need to make sure that the person you are working with is someone that you trust, who is honest, and looks out for your best interest.

In my business, we are a CPA firm. However, we also provide education for financial literacy. Believe it or not, because of the financial literacy piece, we are considered to be high risk. To me, it really doesn't make sense. I would think accounting errors would incur higher risks. But, this is what we were told. Because of this, we had a shorter list of companies who would even write insurance for us.

Therefore, more demand, less supply. In our particular case, our insurance is higher. This happens depending on what products and services you provide.

This is why it is critical that your agent understands your exact need.

You want someone who is willing to go through the process. But, who knows your life best and your business the best? *You do*. Sometimes an insurance company don't necessarily understand. Therefore, it is critical to understand what is in your policy.

And if you are a business, write down exactly the kind of services you provide. Because once they write the policy, those services are going to be covered, unless there's exclusions to them. The description of services is extremely important.

Whether personal or for business, make sure you get what you need.

Building Financial Language:

When selecting a policy and provider, what are you looking for from your agent?

____

____

____

____

____

____

____

7 Homeowner’s Insurance

Watch video

https://youtu.be/hUDVbthxVQk

You would think homeowners insurance would be relatively easy to purchase. But it comes with its own set of complexities. Depending on what state you’re in, and if that state is known for natural disasters, it can become more expensive. Certain companies may not even want to write policies in certain states. I live in Florida and have found this to be true. Due to frequent damage from storms and hurricanes, many providers don’t want to take the risk.

> When it comes to homeowner’s insurance, the primary value is the building itself.

They place value on what it would take to replace it if there was a claim. From their perspective, they want to make the value is higher in order to make sure that they are paid enough. The higher the valuation, the higher the insurance premium.

There’s two schools of thought when it comes to property valuation. Some homeowner’s want the value to be higher and are okay paying a higher premium.

From a replacement value perspective, they want to know they can be made whole through a claim.

The other school of thought seeks to reduce value on the policy since it raises the cost. These individuals may only seek insurance because a mortgage lender requires it. They seek out the lowest price possible. A word of caution. Though the premium may go down, the property may not be properly insured. Reducing coverage allows you to lower costs, but it doesn't mean you have the necessary protection.

Always get the necessary protection.

One thing to note, where there may be room to negotiate, is the fact that these policies look at the building and then take a percentage of the building to estimate the value of contents. If you have a building worth $400,000 and they use a 25% estimate for contents, they ensure $100,000 worth of contents. If that same building gets rated at $600,000 the next year, the insurance company will require $150,000 in content coverage (25%), although this does not mean you have $150,000 in contents. But that's how the policy works. You have to look at what's being covered and start a conversation from there.

One way to minimize your homeowner's insurance is to do a wind mitigation study. This determines whether or not you had the most current construction and your roof is in good condition. You can earn credits against the cost of the insurance and reduce your premium significantly. But you have to go ahead and do that study in order to find out if you qualify for a reduced rate. When you are proactive you can potentially save thousands of dollars.

Building Financial Language:

What actions have you taken in the past, or might you consider in the future, in order to reduce your homeowner's insurance policy while still being properly insured?

____

____

____

8 Life Insurance Considerations

https://youtu.be/F18gVL5ogtE

Watch video

The thing about life insurance is that we will never be able to collect on it. At least not our life. However, what is it really for? It's not for us. It's for those that need us. They need a replacement for us if we're no longer here. The value that we bring to the family or business is so important that if we're not around, they may not be able to cover their bills. They may have to sell a house or may have to close down a business.

> Protecting them from that happening is what life insurance is all about.

It protects those who are dependent on the insured. From an individual basis, it generally benefits spouses and children. It could support siblings too, depending on your situation. The goal is for these individuals to have enough funds to use in order to continue their lifestyle without any significant changes.

From a business perspective, life insurance is important to make sure your business partners are protected.

If you are the one who is bringing in a significant amount of revenue or billable work, and you don't have a proper amount of insurance or you don't have any life insurance, it may force that business to shut down.

In terms of how you purchase life insurance or exactly what policies, there's a term policy just for insurance and then there are separate policies that include insurance and investment.

These may include group variable, universal life insurance, straight line insurance, straight line paid up, and more. Those policies build cash value. Where term policies are solely for insurance. It's an expense. You pay it, and it's done.

For policies which are investment tools plus insurance, the goal is to put money in and it will continue to build. From here, you can elect, as you build cash value, to let the cash value pay for the policy.

Building Financial Language:

Who does or who would benefit from you holding a life insurance policy?

____

____

Are you more interested in a investment policy or solely an insurance policy? And why?

____

____

____

Your Take Action Challenge

https://youtu.be/NSmrZIk5Qxo

Watch video

Your risk management Take Action Challenge is to list of all the different types of insurance policies you would consider in order to manage your risk. Consider this from both a business side and a personal side. Remember, there are a lot of insurance options.

As you start, think about how you're going to protect those you care for and the items that you value, in order to be able to be made whole if there is a loss.

Think of the made whole perspective.

The goal is to be made whole. Some individuals may get a windfall of funds that they may not need and invest it. If that happens for them, this is great. But at the end of the day, it's about covering a loss. That's why you purchase insurance.

Our challenge to you is to make a list of all of the different policies you may need and attach a reason to why you are getting that insurance. Define what you are protecting and what you want to be made whole.

Your Take Action Challenge:

What is one person or thing that you value:

___

What protection can you put in place to be made whole if there is a loss to that person or thing?

___

___

What is another person or thing that you value:

___

What protection can you put in place to be made whole if there is a loss to that person or thing?

___

___

What is one more person or thing that you value:

___

What protection can you put in place to be made whole if there is a loss to that person or thing?

___

___

MONEY MATTERS UNIVERSITY

EQUIPPING YOU TO RETAIN WEALTH

Discussion #20

Avoiding Scams

Discussion #20

Avoiding Scams

Discussion #20

Avoiding Scams

The Big Idea:

Putting personal practices in place,
gives us a better chance of avoiding a scam.

Avoiding Scams

Watch video

https://youtu.be/k4QFNkRa0s4

I was at a hotel for work and I used the Wi-Fi there. It was supposed to have great security, and there didn't seem to be any problems during my stay. A few days after I came back, I got a phone call to say my system had been hacked. This was a legitimate call, a co-worker with my company. He told me: Two weeks ago, we have records of emails coming in and out of your account from 70 different countries.

Well, I didn't travel overseas. I simply went to one hotel in the northeast. I don't know what happened or how the hacker got in. But, I decided from that point on, that I would not use public Wi-Fi anymore. I'd rather use my own phone and open a hot spot so I have a secure network. If I'm just watching a movie or something, that is fine. But for work or any transmission of data that is personal, I will not use public Wi-Fi.

Email access and banking info are sensitive information. You can get hit with fraud or a scam.

Fortunately, my team caught the breach. We shut it down, and it was over. But it reminds me of how easy it can be for someone to get into our systems.

I receive constant messages from people seeking to start a conversation. They will ask: "How's business going?" Or, "Hey, you missed your Zoom call." But is that legit or not? It has been hard for us to always tell. *Why*? Because we're constantly looking for new business. We want people to use our company's services. But in doing so, we are vulnerable to start a relationship with someone who is attempting a scam.

Unfortunately, most of the engagement we get from those we do not know is not good engagement. But it is not always clear initially because it looks like someone wants business services.

I'm in a public environment. People can see who we are. Yet, I don't really know whether or not I'm being hacked or someone is trying to defraud me or it's scam.

Here is the first red flag. As soon as somebody asks for money, you know it's a scam. That's not the way new and genuine relationships work.

In the instance at the hotel, we were fortunate to be able to shut that down. Some things are not that simple. Sometimes people get into things without you realizing, and then you have a big problem. This can happen in the work world and personal world. It even happens in the dating sites. Even the best people are at risk of being hacked.

That's why it is important for us to stay aware and vet each and every type of relationship, be it business or personal.

Building Financial Language:

Has someone disingenuous ever reached out to you or someone you know? How did you know it was a scam attempt? And how did you resolve it?

____

____

____

____

2 Scam Red Flags

Watch video

https://youtu.be/Bq74fzvk9Fo

When it comes to scams, the first red flag is when someone asks you for money. Why would they be asking you for money? If it's somebody you don't know, and they're asking for money, the simple truth is you should not send them funds.

You need to validate anybody you communicate with.

I think it was a lot easier when I was young. Back then, we made friends with people we wanted to be friends with. We knew who they were. We went to school with them. They were in the neighborhood. Some people you liked, some you didn't like.

If you came to me and wanted to be my friend, and I didn't want to be your friend, I didn't have to let you get close to me. Or maybe over time, I'd become your friend because I got to know you. The way it is in the digital world, all we see is someone's name. Even the picture could be fake. We are just interacting with a persona.

So how do we protect ourselves?

As an example, in the online dating world, it is especially difficult to know who someone is and what their intentions are.

Here are a couple of signs to be careful for no matter who you are talking to. The first thing is if somebody asks you to go to a different site to start to communicate. Many times they want to move the conversation to WhatsApp or a Google text, but they do not want to video chat.

They have a means to isolate you in these forums. Why do they want this? Because they want to make sure you are in a controlled environment. That's one sign. It's very subtle, but it's the first sign.

The second sign is you can never call them. Every time you try to call them, it doesn't work. They may call you. But you can't call them.

Anytime someone is seeking to learn about you and tell you what you want to hear, this is a warning sign. Before you know it, they ask for money or personal information. Never give away your Social Security number. And even if your name and address or phone number could be found in public record, there's no need to provide that in any form of a new relationship.

Scammers have a goal in mind. Whatever that goal is, they're going to push for you to give them that. There's an ask at some point. It ends up being money most of the time. But it could be anything. Unfortunately, you have to realize these are real issues that any of us could face. Therefore, these are things we have to be careful about.

Building Financial Language:

What red flags alert you that you are in danger of being scammed?

____

____

____

____

3 Top Tips To Protect Yourself From Being Scammed

https://youtu.be/qZUV6JFYUHA

Watch video

The best way to protect yourself from a scam is to minimize giving out personal information. Additionally, I recommend checking your accounts on a regular basis. That might mean looking at your bank account on a daily or weekly basis to ensure all of the transactions that have hit are valid transactions.

It is crucial to protect your access. This includes keeping your login and passwords private. Never give that information to anybody you do not trust 100%. Make sure you avoid entering any of that information on a public machine or open network.

Scammers wait for an opening. Somebody else could hack your devices over Wi-Fi. There are certain tools that allow someone who is waiting to catch your information when it is transmitted on a public network. They could pull it and take it from you easily.

My best advices is to change your passwords on a regular basis. Rotate them as best as you can. Multi-factor authentication is great because it forces two separate things like a password and a PIN number to allow access.

Another tool I like to use? Alerts. Meaning, if your bank goes under a certain amount, make sure you get an alert, a notification. Set up a control so if an activity or a transaction is greater than a certain dollar amount, you get an alert.

Make sure you prepare in advance. This means you're not reacting, you're being proactive.

Building Financial Language:

What tools do you use to protect your accounts?

___

___

___

Is there an additional alert or control you would like to start using? When might you be able to set that up this week?

___

___

___

___

___

4 If You Think You Have Been Scammed...

https://youtu.be/VsoSUROSNUM

Watch video

If you think you've been scammed, the very first thing you need to do is to call that bank, credit card company, or funding institution—to inform them of the situation. Make sure you call them directly.

Make sure they're valid and that the agent is an actual representative of that institution. If it's a bank account that has been breached, call your banker. If it's credit card company, check the back of the card and use that phone number. If it has something to do with payroll, call your employer. If it's something to do with insurance, call your insurance agent.

Unfortunately, if your bank account or credit card has been hacked, they can freeze your account instantly. Once you call them, they'll ask questions such as, "Do you have the card in front of you? Is this a charge you recognize?"

If you don't have the card, or don't recognize that charge, they're going to cancel your card. And boom, it's canceled immediately.

Once it's canceled, that's an issue.

It is going to be a disruption to your financial life for a while. That is why I recommend putting controls in place to minimize these risks. Otherwise, it's going to take quite some time to recover.

Consider putting new alerts and new processes in place to minimize the risk of this happening in the first place, or from ever happening again.

Fortunately, if you do have a situation where somebody has defrauded you, generally you will be supported by the bank and the credit card company. They will work with you to make you whole and get your funds back.

However, if you take action on your own, such as accidentally responding to an email or you make a payment for something of your own free will, you may not get that back. But if somebody hacks into your account, out of your control, you most likely will be made whole.

Just know—it is going to be a process.

Building Financial Language:

Do you know someone who has had their account hacked? If so, what process did they have to go through in order to recover? How long did that process take?

____

____

____

____

____

5 Relationship Scams

https://youtu.be/PFnOP9YhvmA

Watch video

Scams are getting more and more sophisticated as we advance in the digital age. With all of our communication options today, it is easy for others to target a person. *Why*? Because it is easy to find information about each other online. Think about how easy it is to find where someone lives, who their family is, what kind of job they have, where they've worked, and so on. This makes it easy for them to reach out to you and start a conversation as if they know you.

Recently, someone messaged me on LinkedIn and started by saying, "I see we are both connected to "so and so" on LinkedIn, how do you know them?"

This was a ploy to try to hook me into a sense of trust.

In a scam, the way in is often through relationships. They're going to find out what's important to you. They're going to make it feel like you can trust them. You don't even know who they are, but it is easy to think they're a nice person. But, *what makes them nice*? Just because they know a lot about you doesn't mean they care. It just means they put time in to research you.

I remember interviewing somebody once for a position in my company. The person came in with a stack of papers. They had pulled information on our website about the company and printed it all out. He pretty much threw the papers at me as if I was supposed to be impressed. The question is, did he read it? Did he understand it? He was trying to make a connection, but did so poorly.

That's what happens online. People say they care, but before you know it, you're connected with someone that's not who you think they are. That's the key.

> You think you're connected, but you have a relationship with something that's not real.

That's a scam. It is something to avoid. Be careful. Get face to face if you can, or get other people to endorse the connection. Someone may have just pulled info off of your profile.

What am I really advocating for? For you to be safe. Unfortunately, there's a lot of bad people out there. They take advantage, so be really careful. Never be afraid to delete and block someone who has poor intentions towards you. Delete and block. Sometimes I'll even report. Delete, block, report. Whatever options I have. It's fine to go ahead and block somebody. You must protect yourself so that they don't come after you on a regular basis.

Building Financial Language:

What tactics have you seen when it come to building a fake relationship?

____

____

____

____

____

____

6 Two Types Of People

https://youtu.be/2Ebwjxfwb5w

Watch video

Fundamentally, I believe that there are two types of individuals. You have those that tell the truth and those that don't tell the truth. You have those that care about doing the right thing, and you have those who don't.

Let's break this down a little bit. What's the problem with that? The problem is: It is easy to get hurt if our belief system is contrary to someone else's.

I personally believe in telling the truth. I think it's really important to be an honest individual. I believe that if you're honest it comes back to you. Some may not believe this, but it is what I believe.

But there is a paradigm at play here.

When I talk to someone and I tell the truth, I also believe that they tell the truth. *Why*? Because those that tell the truth think everybody tells the truth. We tend to believe the way we think is how other people think. We wouldn't know any different.

Conversely, people that *don't* tell the truth think that anyone they are conversing with are *not* telling the truth.

This means that when I tell the truth, I think you're telling the truth. But you're not. And you think I'm lying. But you're lying. Who's going to suffer the most on this one? The person that's telling the truth is at a higher risk of being taken advantage of.

Have you ever heard someone say that a person they knew was always at risk of getting conned? That's because this individual tells the truth and can't get over the fact that there are people that don't tell the truth.

That's hard to learn.

Unfortunately, it's easier to believe after you have experienced it. However, my recommendation is to not change as a person. You be who you are. Just don't let somebody else make you who you're not. That, to me, is the fundamental difference between those two individuals.

How do we protect ourselves? We must put guardrails in place. If you think somebody's not telling the truth, ask questions. Seek clarity. Share your concerns with a trusted friend.

Building Financial Language:

Are you trusting or suspicious of others, and why?

Your Take Action Challenge

Watch video

https://youtu.be/tBa8Wm7IbLU

Here is the challenge I have for you. I want you to make a list of anything you to log in with that has a user name and password.

Then, I want you to find a software product to place all of your logins and passwords in. Keep them all in one spot. Some of these software packages are free. Do some research on what works best for you. I happen to use Password Keeper®. It works great for me.

Go through this process of making the list.

Obviously it needs to be secured. And even with that, some people may hesitate to want to do that. The thinking is that if somebody gets in there, that person will have access to all of their passwords and logins. But these tools have controls for that. Often, it is a site where you can rotate passwords on a regular basis. They typically use multi-factor authentication.

One of the best things you can do is start to rotate passwords. Come up with some sort of a plan for your passwords. Pick a base name and numbers or characters. Create your own system.

Many of these programs will ask you to change passwords every three to six months. That becomes really difficult to manage.

It may be tempting to put it on a spreadsheet or write it on paper or put it in your phone under contacts or notes.

To me, that is too risky. Instead, I would recommend coming up with a formal system. That's what we'd like you to do in terms of taking action.

Building Financial Language:

What software program did you find that works best for your needs?

____

____

____

Do not write your formal system here. Instead, consider what plan you can use to rotate your passwords easily.

____

____

____

Discussion #21

Identity Theft

Discussion #21

Identity Theft

Discussion #21

Identity Theft

The Big Idea:

Our personal information and financial story is worth protecting.

1 What Is Identity Theft?

Watch video

https://youtu.be/XsOw-adT86E

Identity theft happens when someone assumes your identity, meaning they use your information to impersonate you in some shape or form. This information is often used to benefit them financially. However, they might use your information to get certificates, or even to obtain licensing. For the purpose of today's discussion, we're going to only focus on the financial side.

There was a TV show in the 80's called Remington Steele. Remington Steele was about a female private detective, Laura Holt. However, when she started her agency, she couldn't get any work because she was a woman. Remember, this was the 80's. At that time, wrong as it was, it was culturally the norm to only hire men for those kind of jobs. So Laura decided to create a fictitious persona. She called that person Remington Steele. *Mr*. Remington Steele.

Now, of course, nobody ever met Mr. Remington Steele. She just named her firm after him. Then she would meet clients and solve the case. Her clients always wanted to meet Mr. Remington Steele, but she never had to introduce him because she found creative ways to camouflage the fact he didn't exist.

In the plot of the TV show, Pierce Brosnan, the actor who ultimately became Mr. 007 himself, enters the story. He is a bit of a con guy with a lot of swagger. He sees what Laura is doing and decides to make a connection with her. He knew right away what she was doing. So guess what he did? *He* became Remington Steele. He took over the identity of the persona she had created in order to get business. Now this is a TV show and obviously is not what we're talking about when it comes to identity theft. However, he saw an opportunity to take a position where he could present himself as something that he's not.

That's what identity theft is.

Of course, none of us want that to happen. It has not happened to me, however, when it occurs, it's difficult to make sure everything is managed properly and that you can be made whole.

This is why it is important to protect your identity and your personal information and to check yourself on a regular basis.

Building Financial Language:

In your own words, how would you define identity theft?

____

____

____

____

____

____

____

____

How Identity Theft Has Evolved

https://youtu.be/65XOTwSYKfs

Watch video

Regardless of technology, there will always be those who will attempt something illegal. Stealing an identity is one strategy they use. Their goal is to get to our personal information and use it to their advantage.

A long time ago, when credit cards were relatively new, individuals stole your identity, or rather stole your credit card's identity, by create their own credit card with your numbers.

There were these machines we used to use in the 80's and 90's which captured your credit card numbers when you went to pay. All of these credit cards had numbers on them which were raised. Credit cards were placed, at point of sale, into this flat machine. You would place a piece of carbon copy paper on top of the card. This would create the credit card receipt after you swiped the top of the machine over the card, in order to record the numbers on the receipt.

The vendor would enter the credit card information after the sale in order to get their money from the company. Today, credit card numbers are not raised. They're just flat. And the sale is not made through a carbon copy impression on a receipt. Everything's electronic. But back then, someone could take a blank piece of paper and copy the numbers. Then, they would actually create their own credit card. Or, they might simply save the numbers to call and place an order with someone else's numbers that they took.

All you needed in order to buy something was the 16 digits. There was nothing else to validate a sale. There were no magnetic tapes, no chips, no validation.

After this became a huge problem, credit cards were designed with magnetic tapes on them. In order to pay, you would swipe the credit card through the machine and it read the tape to get your account numbers.

Hackers got smart. They put a tiny device in the tape reader to grab the numbers and save that information to use as they pleased. Again, they created their own little magnetic tape tied into that particular credit card.

Ultimately, this led to credit card companies creating the chip in the cards like we have today. I think the chip tends to be better. And now, we have tap to pay.

Even though we are become more advanced and seeking to protect ourselves more and more, there's always a way for someone to steal personal information. It's much more sophisticated now since everything is more tech heavy. But we can be incredibly vulnerable online. We have to be careful that nobody is cloning our information.

My point? As things evolve, we have to evolve those measures. We must be vigilant to protect ourselves.

Building Financial Language:

What regular practices do you use to protect your information?

____

____

____

3 My Story

https://youtu.be/1X3HR1AVJTs

Watch video

Fortunately, I have never had my identity stolen. However, my credit card has been hacked.

I grew up in New York where Citibank was a major bank. On almost any corner, you could find a Citibank ATM. One night, I was pulling out a little bit of money, and I thought to myself that I should check the balance on my Citibank credit card that was linked to my Citibank banking account. It was an odd thought to have, because even though I had that credit card, I never used it. But I hit the button to check all of my balances, and it said my balance owed was $4,000.

I was shocked.

I thought it was wrong. I thought it was telling me that was my the credit line. But no. When I checked again it said my balance owed was $4,000. I went home to call Citibank and the story started to unfold.

Here is what happened. Somebody got access to my credit card. They called my credit card company and had my address changed so that they would receive my banking mail. After they changed my address and they started to get mail at the address, they had a card issued in their name. Then they took a trip to Atlantic City and spent $4,000 in one trip. They probably took all the money out as chips.

The entire time, I had no idea.

They changed the address, so I didn't get any mail. I had no way to know the address had been changed. I was never going to get another statement. Then they added a card, which of course I could not have known because the address was changed. Then they charged it, which again I wouldn't known unless I checked my balance at an ATM, which I did by accident.

By the time I found out, the account was delinquent already, and my credit score was impacted.

When I spoke to Citibank, they sent me to the fraud department. The good news was that they made me whole. They credited everything back. They absolutely understood that someone had stolen the identity of my credit card. Everything got resolved.

However, this taught me that I need to check my credit card balances regularly. I need to check my bank balances regularly. Sometimes, it is the only way to catch if there is an error or fraudulent situation. If you get yourself into these healthy financial habits it can help you know if someone has attempted to assume your identity or misuse your information.

Building Financial Language:

How often do you think you need to check all of your accounts in order to remain aware of the activity happening in each one?

____

____

____

____

4 Common Ways Identity Theft Happens

Watch video

https://youtu.be/NIDuquQHAOE

Stealing identity goes beyond getting into credit cards. Anything that has a personal identification can be a target. This might be a driver's license, passport, Social Security number, your name, address, and phone numbers, or any potential logins or passwords you have.

The other thing which is rarely talked about—is your tax return. That one document has a ton of information on it. If someone were to get access to your tax returns, they also know your Social Security number and a great deal of other personal information.

That's another reason why I recommend filing a tax return electronically. There is less threat of leaving a paper trail. Instead, it goes directly from a preparer right to the IRS. Just be careful. A tax preparer has access to your personal information. Simply vet out who you hire to prepare your taxes. Make sure they're trustworthy.

You don't really know who's preparing your taxes when you walk into a retail tax preparer. You just go in and give someone your information.

I'm not sure I would be comfortable with that.

But who you go to for your tax preparation service is something you need to decide.

Other ways that identity theft happens includes hacking into computer systems. If they hack into a computer system, they can steal data on the hard drive. This is why it is crucial that we protect our work and personal devices. Only well-trusted individuals should be able to access our information, and only for the right reason.

In all of the information we are sharing with you here, we are not seeking to create fear. We do not want you worried or upset or afraid that you will be targeted. Instead, we see it as very important for you to understand where the vulnerabilities are. Our objective is to make sure you're well-informed, so you are protected.

Building Financial Language:

When was the last time that someone asked you for highly personal information and what was the reason they asked?

____

____

____

In that situation, what steps did you take to protect your information, or would you like to take the next time a similar situation occurs?

____

____

____

Indicators Of Identity Theft

Watch video

https://youtu.be/0fu2Eo6yJVM

You might wonder: “How would I know if I’m a victim of identity theft?”

There are certain indicators. The first would be getting a bill or an email about an item that you didn’t purchase. You could get a call from someone trying to collect a debt that you know nothing about.

Another hint would be if you were to apply for a loan and it was denied, or they report your credit score is lower than you thought it was. That’s usually an indicator that there’s something else going on.

You could end up with a non-sufficient funds notice or see that your checks are starting to bounce.

Sometimes, someone will receive unexpected medical bills from doctors and medical institutions that they do not even know.

If your utilities are shut off, you may want to check to see if the bill got paid.

If you have difficulty signing into your financial accounts, you will want to check to see if there is any unknown activity. If you receive new credit cards in the mail that you did not authorize, or if you have negative information about your credit reports, these are also indicators of identity theft.

If any one of these things happens, it doesn't automatically mean somebody has stolen your identity. But something didn't happen that should have, or something happened that shouldn't have.

It simply means it is time to look into it and make sure that you have a chance to protect yourself if there is activity happening in your name that you did not authorize.

Building Financial Language:

Has something ever looked off in one of your accounts and you had to investigate what happened? Share that story.

____
____
____
____
____

How did that incident get resolved?

____
____
____
____

6 Who Is Most Vulnerable?

Watch video

https://youtu.be/C0moUUI4TvY

Who do you think is at most risk of identity theft?

The first group that comes to mind, for me, is definitely the elderly. When somebody is older, they are an easy target. It's sad to say that hackers will sometimes look at obituary notices to see if a spouse passes. They know the surviving spouse has become more vulnerable now that they are on their own.

But it doesn't necessarily mean you have to be old to be targeted. It could be someone younger, but the older individuals tend to be at a higher risk. Especially because they may not have family around to help them navigate an attempt.

That's when they're at the most risk.

Someone that is younger is also an easy target, simply because they are not as familiar with fraudulent tactics and threats. If they have never had someone purposely try to take advantage of their personal information, they're simply more vulnerable. They just may not realize that there are people out there that are looking for an easy target.

Unfortunately, the reality is that we are all vulnerable. Some of us are a little more than others. However, we are all vulnerable.

This is why we must take action to
put things in place to protect ourselves.

Building Financial Language:

In your view, who is most vulnerable and why?

7 How To Protect Yourself

Watch video

https://youtu.be/JJ05jYxC4lU

One of the best practices to protect yourself is to rotate passwords for your online accounts.

And if you receive mail with any personal information on it, do not just throw it away. I would highly recommend you shred it. I shred everything. I even shred envelopes because I just don't want to take the risk of any information being out there for others to see.

If you have an old credit card that has expired, shred it or break it up. Cut it with scissors. It may seem extreme, but I even put different pieces of the cut up card in different garbage pails and make sure the garbage goes out at different times. I am that detailed when it comes my credit card. *Why*? Because the numbers are still on the card. While that three digit or four digit security code will change and so will the expiration date, it's still the same account number. And I don't want anyone having that.

Next, always make sure that when you're on a computer that you know it is on a trusted network. If it's an environment with a Wi-Fi that is not an open Wi-Fi, just be aware of who is protecting it.

In our office, we have Wi-Fi for our clients. We connect them happily and are okay with them using our Wi-Fi so we can help them share documents and data quickly. But we know our security and what is in place so that our system is safe.

I would not, however, take my work laptop to an open Wi-Fi network and begin working on their personal information in an open environment. That would not be wise.

Next, if someone calls you out of the blue and they start to tell you information about you that is accurate, don't automatically assume that they're who they say they are simply because they have that information. If you ever feel like that person is not who they say they are, end the call and call the company who they said they were representing. Initiate the call yourself and verify with a representative directly.

These days, it is to easy for someone to seek to defraud you by seeking to make you think they're an official individual from a bank or a credit card company.

Lastly, always make sure that you're monitoring your credit reports on a regular basis and have eyes on all activity that has transpired over the last few months.

Building Financial Language:

What measures do you currently use to protect yourself from fraud and identity theft—and what new ones would you like to start using?

____

____

____

____

8 Recovering From Identity Theft

Watch video

https://youtu.be/3W__wFSXuHo

If you've discovered that you are a victim of identity theft, know that this situation can be managed. While this is serious, there is no need to panic. There are steps that can be taken.

First, you must make sure that you resolve everything that has already happened, meaning we must recover from whatever damage was done in terms of credit cards or bank accounts. This means that the first thing to do is to call those institutions to get cards and accounts canceled or frozen.

After that, there will be time to try to figure out what happened and where the thief got in.

Take a personal assessment and ask how you might be able to mitigate that risk in the future. This takes us back to risk management. We are always learning and growing, asking ourselves, "How do I make it better to minimize risk in the future?"

The truth is, even with the best securities in place, you may not be able to eliminate it. I had a credit card for my business that got hacked. My bank replaced my card. Three months later, it happened all over again.

I had nothing to do with it.
And you may not either.

They changed the account number and cards. I had to do it all over again. And that's why I decided to get two cards. One that I only use for online purchases and one that I use for day-to-day purchases in stores.

I am always looking to make changes that help keep my information safe. *My advice*? Make tweaks in order for it to be easier to stay safe. Protect yourself with best practices. And make sure that when you need help that you connect with those who can help you become whole and guide you with tips and tools to know how to make it better in the future.

Building Financial Language:

If you were to face a situation in which you believe your information was stolen and used improperly, what would you do first?

Your Take Action Challenge

Watch video

https://youtu.be/ffTVHqSkTMU

If you've never had your identity stolen, that's wonderful. My question to you is:

How can you stack the deck on your side to prevent identity theft from ever happening to you?

Take some of the information we've discussed in this lesson and define what plan you're going to put together in order to make sure you protect yourself from being vulnerable to identity theft.

Building Financial Language:

My personal protection plan is:

One thing I am going to stop doing is:

Steps I am going to take this week in order to protect myself include:

MONEY
MATTERS
UNIVERSITY
EQUIPPING YOU TO RETAIN WEALTH

Discussion #22

Entrepreneurship

Discussion #22

Entrepreneurship

Discussion #22

Entrepreneurship

The Big Idea:

Entrepreneurship allows a visionary who has discipline and business acumen a chance to bring their ideas to life and change the world.

What Is Entrepreneurship?

Watch video

https://youtu.be/7B-UdOQ3UcU

What is entrepreneurship? Entrepreneurship is when an individual decides to go into business and many of them have little to no fear about what they want to do.

They have ideas and they're going to see them actualized in an independent way.

They don't necessarily want to work for someone.
They want to work for themselves.

Their goal? They want to create something that has potentially never been created before. Most of them have a tremendous amount of talent and vision.

You would consider an entrepreneur to also be an opportunist. When they see something, they're ready to take action.

Building Financial Language:

In your own words, how would you define an entrepreneur?

____

____

____

____

____

____

Who can you think of that embodies an entrepreneurial spirit?

____

____

____

____

____

____

If you could bring any idea or vision to life, what would you create?

____

____

____

____

____

____

Traits Of Great Entrepreneurs

Watch video

https://youtu.be/fPk4QnpVacA

What are the traits of an entrepreneur? They have very little fear. They're ready to go and try something. They're very comfortable in their skin and confident about what they believe in.

Even if they may have a bit of trepidation, it doesn't matter because they know they can always find a way through the challenge.

They are true opportunists.

They're ready to move at any time. If they see an opportunity, they're going to jump at it. Even if it doesn't necessarily make sense to the average person, they will move toward it if it fits the vision they have.

Being an entrepreneur is not for the faint of heart. Great entrepreneurs have to be able to let things go and move on.

One thing I want to clarify is that an entrepreneur is not necessarily conservative or aggressive. You can be an entrepreneur and be conservative. An entrepreneur is someone that makes a decision to move forward in a business idea. But how they run the business is different.

There's a very big distinction between the two.

Let's not get confused. Just because somebody is super aggressive does not mean they're a great entrepreneur or that they are an entrepreneur at all. An entrepreneur is someone that wants to have their own business. They want to be able to control what's happening in their environment. And they happen to be some of the most innovative individuals.

Many of them want to and do
change their corner of the world.

Building Financial Language:

What traits or character qualities come to mind when you think of entrepreneurs?

____

____

____

____

____

A Chance To Change The World

https://youtu.be/AEXWwVFJu7k

Watch video

When I think of entrepreneurs, I tend to think of individuals that have changed the world and how they did it. For example, electricity changed the world. The invention of the telephone changed the world. Today, the internet, social media, and technology continues to change the world almost daily.

Many years ago, the railroad changed our world. Airplanes changed the world. There's so many individuals who were behind these inventions, and many of them were entrepreneurs. There are too many to mention their names. But it leads me to wonder:

What do you see as possible?
What can you do?

That's really the question. Are *you* an entrepreneur?

Do you have ideas?

I know it is not easy to bring an idea to life. I know that many inventors and dreamers who seek to bring something new into the world have faced a tremendous amount of hardship through most of their life.

When it comes to inventors as opposed to an entrepreneurs, unfortunately many of them never saw the full fruits of their work or got much wealth out of it.

An inventor creates something.
An entrepreneur sees how it's going to change the world.

The inventor works for the entrepreneur. Where the entrepreneur is seeking to create a shift in the world.

Building Financial Language:

Do you see yourself as an employee, a leader, a business owner, an inventor, an entrepreneur, or a blend of any of these? And why?

____

____

____

____

____

4 The Confidence It Takes

https://youtu.be/K5YfeHhRc84

Watch video

An entrepreneur needs a pretty good amount of confidence because they have to believe in themselves. Unfortunately, not many may believe in them. Especially if they haven't created anything yet. It is tough to get buy in with new innovation since it is something no one has seen before.

The first thing most people tend to say when an idea is brought up is, "Well, nobody did that before. I don't know if it will work." I can't stand that perspective.

Entrepreneurs often feel alone and will question themselves. But in front of others, they will be confident. *Why*? Because they know if they aren't confident in their idea, they're not going to get support. And they ultimately need support.

Entrepreneurs are motivators.

They're so confident in what they believe that others get excited because there's so much energy. Others want to be part of it. Does it mean everything is always happy and perfect? No. There will always be setbacks and challenges.

There's going to be failure. But entrepreneurs see failure as a sign that something didn't work rather than something being over. They say to themselves: Let's try something different. In order to know how to do something right, you often have to do it "wrong" first.

The first year I became an accountant, I couldn't do anything right. Then, after time, certain things started to change. It started to become natural. It is part of the process. And entrepreneurs know that.

Joe Torre was manager of the New York Yankees. He had an entrepreneurial spirit and great vision. One of the things he introduced to the team was what you call a setup and a closer.

Previously, if a team had a really good pitcher, they would just keep the pitcher in for all nine innings until the game was over. But Joe Torre created this system for there to be one pitcher who was your starter who only had to pitch six innings, not nine innings. He believed there was a better chance for that pitcher to get through six innings without giving up too many runs. *Why*? Because as a game goes on, you may get stronger as a pitcher, but you're pitching more and more. You were also giving the opposing team a chance to learn your style. The longer a pitcher was in the game, the more the batter got to see them pitch.

So Joe waited six innings and then he would bring in another pitcher, which was called the set up pitcher. Then he'd bring in the closer for the ninth inning. This method changed the entire game.

For a long time, the Yankees were a very strong team with that particular system that Joe created.

Now Bill Walsh was a football coach for the San Francisco 49ers. He developed the West Coast offense. In this method, instead of throwing long, deep passes, the team used these short passes. They'd just go out, claim a few yards and throw the pass quick. Defense would drop back and the offense would get three, four, five yards.

Then another five yards and another five yards. They just worked their way down the field. This method changed football.

You do not have to create a light bulb in order to have positive influence. There are many individuals in our society that have small tweaks, little bursts of creativity that end up making huge impact. Before you know it, they're excelling within the new space they created for themselves until everybody catches up to them.

Do you know what happens next?

Somebody else has to come in and make a change to make it even better. *Why*? Because we are constantly improving and constantly learning how to adapt. The world does change. It shifts at the same time. But the visionaries know how to shift and adapt and create with it.

That's is one of the biggest traits of an entrepreneur.

Building Financial Language:

Sometimes an entrepreneur brings a product to life, and sometimes it is a method that changes the world, like Joe did for the Yankees. Is there a method or mindset you would like to introduce to the world? If so, share it here:

____

____

____

____

____

____

____

____

5

Entrepreneurial Decision-Making

https://youtu.be/a5l_nFV4LQg

Watch video

I find it interesting how an entrepreneur makes a decision. I think it's impossible to get into that mindset and know how they made decisions, because every single entrepreneur has their own unique traits when it comes to how they think.

The key, however, is the fact they're willing to make a decision.

In my book, there's only one decision that's a bad decision—and that's indecision. When I would interview an employee, I loved to ask a scenario-based question. I would say: If you were in a situation where you had to make a decision and you did not have all the facts, yet you were the one who *had* to make the decision, what would you do?

Some people answer that they would try to get the facts. To which I challenged: *You don't have time to get all the facts, then what?*

If they wanted to talk to a boss, I would tell them the boss is not available. *At the end of the day, it is on you. That is all you have.*

I know I made many of them uncomfortable, but the truth is, each of us have to decide what we are going to do. We have to make a decision.

In my book, if you're working with me, I want you to make a decision. Use the most amount of information that you have at that moment. Try to make a choice. Understand the basis of why you're making that decision.

To me, whatever happens it's a good decision because you made a choice, even if the results were not necessarily good.

From my perspective, I'm happy to see somebody make a choice. If it lands with a negative result, we can sit down and talk about it. It gives us a chance to say, "What could we have done differently?"

Great leaders know that you have to give somebody the opportunity to try something new without telling them what to do. That's what delegation is all about.

Entrepreneurs don't need to be delegated to. They just go for it.

In a given day, you probably have no idea how many decisions you really make. You make a ton of decisions. We all do. And an entrepreneur is making them fast, sometimes minute-by-minute.

Building Financial Language:

What kind of decision-making process do you use for yourself?

____

____

____

____

6 Testing Your Vision

Watch video

https://youtu.be/PHX8PLpd8_4

We have an exercise I do in workshops. I ask a group of people to sit down, close their eyes, and pick up what's in front of them. Then, I ask them to put whatever it is on. They open their eyes and realize they are looking through prescription glasses. All of a sudden, they are like, "I can't see!"

And do you know why they can't see? Because they are wearing readers! That script is not meant for their eyes. They want to take them off. I mean, have you ever been to the eye doctors when they are trying to match your sight? We go through this exercise of: *I can't see. Oh, let me try these now. Here is another pair. Forget those. This one's not so bad, but it's still not right*. Its frustrating.

And in my case, I'm better off not even using extra lenses, because I don't need them.

The same is true for an entrepreneur.

You see, an entrepreneur doesn't necessarily need to put on the readers. It's built into their eyes. They see the future. They see it as if it is. They have great vision.

They live in the moment and are able to imagine what's going to happen in the future as if it is already happening today. But for others, there's frustration because *you* can't see what *they* see.

Vision is so important. It's where it all starts. I know when it comes to putting business plans together, a lot of individuals state the fact that you need a mission. Next, they want your goals and objectives defined. These are great. But the most important thing is vision. *Why*? Because if you don't start with vision, it is impossible to manifest what you are looking for.

As an entrepreneur, you see that future as if it is. That's great, because you see it. But this is not the end of the road. We have to go to another challenge. Now we have to get support.

One of the most important departments when it comes to deploying a new idea or product is the marketing department. If you create a product or service without consulting or working with a marketing department, you may create something that there's absolutely no market for.

Now I understand that when we're talking about entrepreneurs and new concepts that it may be difficult to see a market if it doesn't exist. But can we create a market? Can we consult with market research, market development, and business development, since they understand that process. *My advice*? Work with them. They need to be brought in to capture data and facts, turn it into usable information, and build a case for you to be able to make a well-informed decision on how to achieve the vision you clearly see.

Building Financial Language:

Why do you think collaboration is so vital when it comes to bringing a new idea to life?

____

____

____

____

____

7 Starting Your Own Business

https://youtu.be/lc9JcUX93BE

Watch video

If you have a vision of the kind of job you want, but you can't find it, what do you think that means? It could mean you are best suited for entrepreneurship.

It's fantastic to have your own business as long as you're the type of person that *can* own a business. I will admit it is not easy. Yet, it is rewarding to define what you want to do and fit that into a market.

My advice:
Learn about your desired market.

Go to network events, especially nonprofit events. If you want to find out about a particular career, find a not-for-profit that has a board of directors who is looking for volunteers. Just get started somewhere.

Start rubbing elbows with the board members. Make sure first and foremost that you have a passion for their mission, and are there to serve. This is not meant to be self-serving, rather a place to test your passion and find out what will give you fulfillment. Never serve just to meet somebody or "get in."

Instead, do your research. Figure it out. Start learning whether or not your aspiration can turn into a career that you can build. Do your homework before you pull the cord, but know this: It is absolutely possible to redefine your career by starting your own business.

Building Financial Language:

Have you ever considered becoming an entrepreneur? If so, what business would you create and who would you provide products or services to?

____

____

____

____

____

8 Getting Started

Watch video

https://youtu.be/5ZgmeNm2FuQ

Let's say you're ready to become an entrepreneur. You have an idea. You're ready to get started. Unfortunately, one of the things we all need is money. But we don't need it to be *our* money. What we really need is *access* to money.

Now, I personally believe that you should financially have skin in the game. In my perspective, when you're willing to put dollars in, somebody else will also be willing to put some dollars in. If you're looking to fund something 100% with someone else's cash, they're going to ask why they are the ones being asked to assume all of the risk.

As an entrepreneur, you need to start to build credibility. If you don't have that yet, you will need to put some skin in the game.

At the end of the day, though, you need to figure out a way to raise money. And that's a talent of its own. You need to be able to pitch your idea yourself and get support.

What you don't want is for partners to look at you as an entrepreneur who does not have a solid foundation. They want to make sure you have ideas put together in a way that is very practical. That's why it is important to create a business plan. This is a very important piece of documentation that creates confidence for others to invest in your ideas, because they understand them. It doesn't take a ton of work to create this plan, but it's very important to be able to present one.

> Within the business plan are the steps that show proof of concept.

Proof of concept means you've tried something and it works. It may be a small sample, but you've tested it. You have had a focus group test your product and give feedback and ideas. Think of a computer program. One method is to test programs before they go out. Alpha version, beta version, and then deployment. An alternative is continuous improvement. It's the same concept. You have to take it step-by-step. There is a very practical aspect to beginning.

Recognize, you don't need to have the entire plan together. You don't have every single step figured out, but you must have the *next* steps.

If you take it one step at a time and can prove what you have is a viable opportunity, then you'll have investors who will want to follow through. Bear in mind, as an entrepreneur, your idea may be so abstract that you will not have a large pool of investors. It may take work for you to find the right people you want as investors. But it is worth it, because these investors, in some shape or form, are really your partners, and you want them to support you.

Building Financial Language:

When you consider the process to get started, what portion seems the most challenging—and who might you be able to partner with to help you meet that challenge?

____

____

____

____

____

9 Be A Lifelong Learner

Watch video

https://youtu.be/PQVv4nAGaks

In your opinion, do you think that entrepreneurs have the ability to listen or that they just want to say what they know or act like they know it all? Or, do you see them as individuals who are open to change?

You might think that because they're creative and are willing to try a lot of things that they would have an open mind. That is what I tend to believe. *Why*? Because they're always looking for opportunities.

I don't like to look at an entrepreneur and pigeonhole them into someone who thinks they know everything. Because a real entrepreneur knows that they don't know everything.

How do they stay that way?
They recognize that there's always room to grow.

One way to grow is to be what we call a *lifelong learner.*

Lifelong learners always want to be better. They always want to improve. It doesn't mean they have to go to school all the time. However, when something comes up or crosses their path, there is curiosity. They are inquisitive, always asking, "What is that? Why are you doing this?"

They just want to learn and absorb something new. They may not know why they want that, but they have an interest. That's why, as an entrepreneur, we need to seek to grow and do new things.

Building Financial Language:

When you think of being a lifelong learner, what are a few ways you can put that into practice that you would enjoy the most?

10 Selecting Your Pricing Model

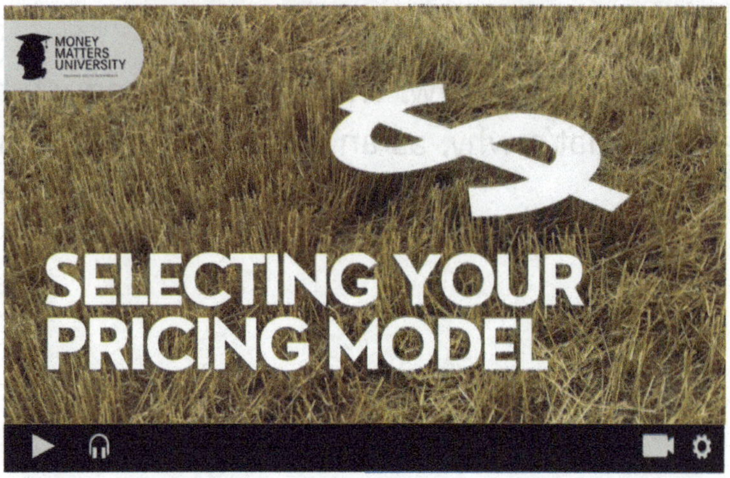

Watch video

https://youtu.be/pufYoHnZ198

When we have a new product, we must price it. One thing to do is see what the competition charges. But how can we do that if it's a new product? There are likely similar elements of that new product that are already in market. Use that as a guideline.

Next, let's look at two different types of pricing. In a for-profit company, meaning it's a business and you want to make money. Just like Stephen Covey says: You start with the end in mind.

Ask yourself: What is the return you're looking for?

How much net profit is the goal once the business is up and running? What is that number? Once you find that, you simply need to build your budget and your business plan around it.

To do so, you need to determine what your infrastructure costs are going to be. How many employees you need? Do you need an office, multiple locations, or additional resources? Think ahead to determine what kind of software and tools and services are going to be necessary to operate your company.

Then you have to recognize that you will have to pay for those operating expenses, and in order to pay for those operating expenses, your gross profit must be at least what your operating expenses are.

You must find your break even.

Once you break even, anything above and beyond that, is profit. This means we must factor in cost to do business and how much revenue we need for the services that we sell or products we offer. The difference between that is your gross profit. Revenue minus cost to sell, is cost of goods sold (or cost of sales), which includes product and labor, equaling your gross profit.

That gross profit now has to be at least your total expenses in order to break even.

Those kind of numbers, and this form of math, is important for an investor. This is why we suggest starting your pricing model from this logic. Because anything above and beyond that is going to be a form of profit.

Theoretically, if we have expenses that are fixed, any additional revenue on top of that is going to be profit. The gross profit will end up going to what we call the bottom line. That's a for-profit business model.

In a not-for-profit business, such as a 501c3, it tends to work the opposite. You share the vision, talk about the mission, get some grants, raise funds, and have a basis to work with.

Instead of starting from the cost basis, you start from a number given to you. Essentially you are given a number which is your revenue. Then you are able to make choices on how to spend the money to fulfill your mission.

This is why a lot of not-for-profits have a beg, borrow, and steal mindset. They have to find volunteers because they can't afford to hire. They don't have enough money coming in.

Instead, they find individuals that love the mission who don't need to get paid.

As an entrepreneur, you can be in the not-for-profit business because there are some entrepreneurs that have wonderful ideas on how to give back to the community.

However, if you're in the for-profit business, you cannot run the business that way. If you run the business that way, you most likely will not succeed.

Therefore, when it comes to the pricing model, you have to understand what your costs are. Once you figure that out, you ask what you need to charge to break even. Working with this method, your cost could be twice of what your competition is, but that's what you need.

This means you not only have to change the world in terms of what you offer, you must also change the paradigm of what people are willing to invest in to get what you're offering.

That's how you set up your pricing model.

Building Financial Language:

When it comes to pricing a product or service, what factors would you choose to help steer your towards a sticker price?

____

____

____

____

____

____

____

____

____

11 Solopreneur or Entrepreneur?

Watch video

https://youtu.be/xm7rg7Nwrlo

What is the difference between a solopreneur and an entrepreneur? It's very simple. The solopreneur is alone, or solo. They do 100% of the tasks within the business. They create the plans. They get the products together. They take care of any infrastructure. They do all administrative tasks, sales, services, and accounting. They do everything. Maybe they outsource a few things to professionals.

However, they pretty much handle it all. The entrepreneur, however, is building an empire. Their objective is to work themselves out of doing everything.

Initially, they cast vision and bring people into the business to achieve the vision. The solopreneur creates the vision and achieves the vision.

Now don't misunderstand. I totally believe an entrepreneur has to have an element of being a solopreneur. *Why*? Because they must understand the steps required to achieve the overall objective.

However, it's temporary.
They only learn to pass on that piece of the puzzle.

Their goal is to bring on quality people who can take the idea to another level.

That's the biggest challenge. Finding the right people. The best way to do that is to make them part of it. Give them a voice on some of the decisions and part of the growth. Give the individuals who are there from the beginning, the rewards of taking your concepts, ideas, and creativity to a new level.

They deserve that just as much as you do,
because you can't grow without them.

And if you're a solopreneur, you will cap out at some point. Burnout is highly prevalent. If burnout happens and you haven't built an infrastructure of individuals to take over, you're probably going to end up shutting the business down.

In the end, that means you were not building an empire, you were building a product for a period of time. Then it ends.

As an entrepreneur, you have a bigger vision. That vision may be to take it to a certain point and then sell it. Or it might be to pass it on to someone else. That's fine. However, you need that infrastructure in order to do either.

That's the main difference between a solopreneur and an entrepreneur.

Building Financial Language:

How would you define the difference between a soloprenuer and entrepreneur? Give an example of each.

___

___

___

___

___

Your Take Action Challenge

Watch video

https://youtu.be/O0L_vjcCBP4

Here is my challenge for you. Let's say you have an idea. Where does that idea come from? It comes from the brain. You have an idea or something you want to do and you think it over. When it becomes really clear to you, then I'm going to ask you to put it on paper or in a diagram.

Bring it out of your head and onto paper. Document your thoughts and ideas.

This is why we say, "I gotta write it down so I get it out of my head." Because there's only so much I know I can hold in *my* brain before I lose the idea. That is why it is crucial to start putting those thoughts on paper.

This does not mean it has to be super formal. Just jot down notes. Ask yourself: What is it that I want to accomplish? What is it that I see as possible in the future? What are you going to create?

Creation #1 happens in the head.
Creation #2 is on paper.

Once you have that, I want you to build a model. Now what does that mean? If it's a product, I want you to build a prototype. If it's a service, I want you to identify the tools you're going to use in the service. I want you to create the prototype of something you would market and sell.

If it's social media, I want you to write a post. If it's something that you're going to deploy or sell I want you to get a visual together in some sort of a model. This is the third creation.

Our first creation was in the head, the second creation is on paper, the third creation is in the form of a product.

The fourth creation is the business itself.

Now we've taken all of our ideas, put it down on paper, created it, and we're closer to being able to actually deploy it. That's my challenge to you, start the process to create your own four-step model.

Building Financial Language:

What is your entrepreneurial idea? And how are you going to take these four steps?

MONEY MATTERS UNIVERSITY

EQUIPPING YOU TO RETAIN WEALTH

Discussion #23

A Business Plan

Discussion #23

A Business Plan

Discussion #23

A Business Plan

The Big Idea:

Setting your goals, while being flexible to the needs of your target audience, give you a North Star for your business.

What Is A Business Plan?

Watch video

https://youtu.be/Z8ulc_UZcG8

Let's talk about a business plan. Let's not make the word "business plan" a stressful thing. Let's make it really simple. The first thing you need to define is what you're offering.

Next, you must define your audience for this product or service. You also need to understand the cost to create what you want to sell and how you're going to distribute it.

If you take these four elements, you can create an outline.

Let's take Money Matters University as an example. Here are the components we have had to think through as we have built our plan.

Our objective is to inform and educate about financial literacy. So our audience includes those who are interested in learning more about financial literacy. However, we've tried to simplify the audience by creating different tracks. This allows us to know our marketing message.

In our business model, we have different audiences. And what are we offering? Education in books and online. However, at the end of the day, we're really providing knowledge and information. How our audience gets that knowledge is not the product. The product is their success in understanding finances and mastering financial literacy in order to make good decisions.

That's what we're really selling.

The book, video, or online service is simply the means by which the product is delivered. However, the way we deliver is part of our business plan.

Then we defined the funding needed. That led us to create our budget.

In a typical business plan, there is an executive summary and information about the product. Fundamentally, that's a business plan.

My advice? Create an outline, determine your cost and selling price, and document your thoughts. Jot that down. Keep in mind: this is your idea, your business, and your passion. Putting it in a document is the final step that puts a bow on it, and makes it ready for somebody to see.

That's your business plan.

Building Financial Language:

What elements do you want to go into your business plan?

____

____

____

____

2 Smart & Stretch Goals

Watch video

https://youtu.be/BlriFpsPLXM

Within the business plan, I think there's two very important components. The first one is a SMART goal. There's five attributes for the word SMART.

"S" means to be very "***Specific***" of what you want to achieve, specific about your goal.

This needs to be "***Measurable (M),***" which means you have to have something to measure against. In some businesses they're called outcomes. Ask yourself: "What is the desired outcome or key result?" That is your measurement.

Make sure it's "***Action-oriented (A).***"

"R" stands for the goal being "***Realistic.***" It's something that can happen. It can't be impossible to achieve.

The **"T"** represents a "***Timeline,***" when you expect results. This can be established through a project manager or milestone.

That's the SMART goal.

When you're putting your goal together, if you make sure each one of these components is part of it, you're going to have something you have a good chance of achieving. To take the SMART goal to another level, I want to talk about what we call a STRETCH goal.

The **"S"** stands for "***Sustainable*** and ***Scalable***." You want to see growth. The **"T"** is to be "***Team-oriented***." You want a full team working on it together. The **"R"** stands for a "***Resolve"*** to make sure the goal gets completed. It speaks to passion within the goal. It carries the attitude of: *I'm totally resolved to make this work*, regardless of whatever it takes.

"E" stands for ***enjoy*** what you do. To me, it's so important to be able to enjoy it. The second **"T"** is to be "***Teachable***." During the process of achieving a goal, you're going to learn a lot of things. No one knows it all. Each of us should be open to learn, and be educated. The **"C"** stands for the fact you "***Care***," you're constantly putting your heart and soul into it.

Finally, the **"H"** is to "***Honor"*** the individuals, the process, and the organization. Altogether, we call this STRETCH for Success.

Between the SMART goals and STRETCH goals, defining those objectives and putting them in your business plan will make it unique. Most business plans will not ask for this kind of clarity, but that's what makes you little different.

You get to take it to another level.

Building Financial Language:

Put a 60-90 minute time slot on your calendar to think through your SMART and STRETCH goals. Who do you want in the room to collaborate with you?

____

____

____

____

Is A Business Plan Fluid Or Static?

Watch video

https://youtu.be/DGWs5-tn6Qk

Sometimes we are asked if a business plan should be static or flexible. Static means it is what it is. The plan doesn't change. Flexible is a plan which is fluid. It can change if something needs to be modified.

I think the plan should include both.

Conventionally, when you put a business plan together, you need to make sure that plan is what you're going to follow. It is something you always have to go back to. Let's call that North. If there are side quests or off the beaten path tangents, we still get back to North.

That's what being fluid means. But what happens if you genuinely need to veer off for a little while? Ultimately yes, you want to come back to your North since that's your core model.

Or is it? Maybe things have changed.

You had to be fluid. Sometimes you had to close down part of the business. Sometimes we pursue a whole new career. Sometimes new markets open up.

So you could have had a plan, but if it isn't going to work, because something from the outside affected your plan, you need room to make new plans.

I don't believe in the conventional wisdom of thinking that when you put a plan together, that you must stick with it, and it can never change. I think that it's really important to be fluid. You can start static, but if you have to shift your model a little bit, and everybody that's involved with the business plan is on board, I think the change is fantastic.

Bear in mind, we're not talking about changing things just because you see something shiny and you are bored with the current plan. Instead, it's a plan that you put together that is allowed to be modified to achieve your initial outcome. *My recommendation*? You need to be flexible in order to do that.

Building Financial Language:

Do you tend to be more of a static or fluid planner? And why?

____

____

____

____

What circumstances do you believe merit change to your original plan?

____

____

____

____

4 When Is The Right Time To Create A Business Plan?

https://youtu.be/Xroi_bhrpns

Watch video

When is the right time to create a business plan? My answer is *today*. Start putting it down on paper. Take notes. I've been taking notes for 30 years. I have little pieces of paper that I wrote many, many years ago. When I look at them, I start to realize there's a consistency in my desire to see something happen.

If you have an idea, write it down. This does not have to be formal at first. But I do recommend putting a business plan together before you launch your business.

Where does the plan begin? It starts in the head, right? You have an idea. Once you have it in your head and you start to write it down, that is actually the beginning of the business plan.

But to get started, you will probably have to get funding. You're going to need a bank and potentially investors. These different organizations will likely ask for your plan to make sure they know you're viable.

One of the things I *don't* want you to do is write a business plan and then put it on a shelf.

You need to do something with the business plan. It's great to make some notes. However, if you want a formal business, you need a document that you can provide for those who want to partner with you.

Letting something sit by itself is never a good idea.

Let's say you're a snowbird. Meaning you pretty much live in Florida six months a year and live someplace else up North for the remaining six months a year. For the six months you're not in Florida, if there is not a plan to tend to your home in the South, what happens to that house in Florida? If you did absolutely nothing and left it dormant, when you come back, something will be broken.

That's what a business plan is like.

If you leave it dormant, and leave it on a shelf, things break down. Things don't work the way you expected them to. When I hear somebody say they are facing an issue in the office, and all of a sudden people start asking, "What's our policy?" It tells me their plan has been on the shelf far too long.

If you need to open up a document to know what to do, you're not using it. Don't make your business plan a trophy. Make your business plan something that you use regularly, something that guides you toward success.

Building Financial Language:

What is the current state of your business plan? And what action would you like to take in order to make it a living document for your organization?

____

____

____

____

____

5 Who Creates A Business Plan?

Watch video

https://youtu.be/hEvYEMg41mQ

The individual who has the initial business idea should start the business plan. But it is okay if that person needs help. They might be the most creative person in the world, however not the best at documenting what they're thinking. This is why we have teams.

In that case, they would need to bring somebody in to work with them. Collectively, they could put that business plan together.

> The vision must radiate throughout the entire business plan.

However, you must make sure that those who are involved are brought in to give input. Otherwise, you're going to end up having something that will not be practical or work.

What you don't want to do is just hire somebody to draft your plan in a generic way. There is no point to sit down with them for a half an hour, tell them what you want and leave them to write a business plan when they do not even know who you are or what you and your team have to offer.

I've seen that happen so many times. Visionaries get frustrated, because the generic plan does not capture exactly what they are thinking. But, they don't share exactly what they're thinking, it's not going to be effective.

You need to get all of those ideas and thoughts out in order to be able to capture them in a document. But the people who help you put it together must be vested. You want them to understand the unique factors and to be part of it. They need to be able to capture the vision and mission you have for the organization.

Building Financial Language:

When considering writing or tweaking your business plan, who do you know that is vested that can capture your unique mission and vision?

6 Who Sees The Business Plan?

https://youtu.be/D7JNBCnvQjI

Now that you have your business plan together, who is going to look at it? Who's going to see it? If you have investors, your investors need to see the plan. A bank also tends to want to see the plan.

These partners want to make sure that you're going to stay solvent. They want to know that they're not making commitments to you that they can't fulfill. The business plan is also for the individuals who are standing behind your company, those who may be signing personal guarantees for lines of credit.

In addition, depending on who you're working with, your vendors and suppliers may be interested in looking at your plan. Sometimes your customers will be interested in your plan. It all depends on the kind of business you're in.

My opinion is that you should have a plan you're very proud of, that you're okay with anybody looking at, and that there are no trade secrets in the plan.

It's simply an indication of how you're going to run your business.

Some parts of your plan need to remain private. However, you need that plan to be available to make sure that everyone who is vested understands the business.

Is it important to let employees see the business plan? *Why not*? Maybe you don't show them detailed financial information. However, they should know what's going on.

If somebody's going to be working for you and they want a career rather than a job, I think it's really important for them to understand the vision of the company.

Go beyond a vision or mission statement. Let them see something beyond what you put on posters throughout the entire office. Eliminate hyperbole.

If you can be true to what you put on the walls, then you would have no reason why you wouldn't be able to show them your plan.

A business plan should be available to all stakeholders. And you get to define who those stakeholders are.

Building Financial Language:

Who are your stakeholders? When was the last time that each party had access to see your business plan?

____

____

____

____

How Does A Budget Fit Into A Business Plan?

Watch video

https://youtu.be/diWe1p0W3t0

How does your budget tie into your business plan? The business plan most likely has milestones. Certain funds are going to be required at certain points in time. You don't necessarily need all of the money up front. But you need funds at a point when you are ready to move to the next step.

Every time there's a milestone, you get to ask yourself the question, "Do I continue, do I stop, or do I modify?"

What does that mean? That means that when you are putting a plan together you put moments in, markers, in which the goal is to achieve certain things in order to continue the plan. This means that your plan may end up stating that you are not going to go forward with the business if it does not get to a certain spot.

And that's okay. You tried something and made the conclusion that it's just not a marketable item, or the cost is too much, or you're not in a position to do it any longer, or the economy and market has changed.

Continue, stop, or modify.

Each business plan will have multiple stages. Some business plans have pre-revenue. This usually exists when there is a need for research and development. Stage one is usually everything required before revenue in order to reach the ability to generate revenue. Stage two is funding. Now, you don't always need to get outside funding. But you do need to put together a budget.

My advice? Define everything you think you're going to need to invest. And as crazy as it may seem, triple that number. We tend to underestimate things. I used to say double the budget. Now I say triple. You may not feel that is necessary, but I would advise you to make sure you have enough money put aside that you *can* triple it. If you don't want to put that in your budget, just make sure it's available.

It would be really sad if you've already invested two thirds of what you need and everything is going well but you run out of money and you have to close. You would have lost everything you invested.

The other thing is: I'm a big proponent of having skin in the game. If you're not willing to invest your money, why would someone else? It is going to be rare for someone to invest without believing there will be a decent return. If you're not going to put skin in the game, my question to you is *why would anybody else*?

When you put your money into the business and create a budget, it sparks accountability to make sure you're reaching those numbers. You have a comparison to actual. Now, they're not going to be the same. They never are. There's always going to be some form of a variance. But that is okay. I need you to look at the business as if the future is now. Not just the business itself, but the finance relative to the business.

Building Financial Language:

How does your budget tie into your business plan?

____

____

____

8 KPIs & OKRs

Watch video

https://youtu.be/rZloDOIQO-4

KPI stands for Key Performance Indicator. A KPI is something that you look at and use to measure the achievements of the company. I'll give you an example. Let's say you have a growing business and your monthly revenue is $10,000 a month, but the goal is to be $15,000 a month. The KPI, Key Performance Indicator, is the monthly revenue.

We want to get to $15,000. We're currently at $10,000, now we're $12,000, now we're $13,000. We hit $15,000, now we reached our indicator. If it goes up or goes down, it tells us what's going on.

Most KPIs are financially driven. However, in certain industries, especially in the not-for-profit world, they call them outcomes. A grant might state that they can get funding if they reach a particular outcome, such as the number of individuals who use the service the not-for-profit offers. That's a KPI.

OKRs stand for Objectives and Key Results.

Objectives are something that are not really measurable. They are qualitative.

For example, my objective is to be the best financial literacy educator in the United States. But how do I measure that? I can't really measure it. But key results are quantitative. That can be measured. So what is the qualitative component of that? It is for Money Matters University to be the largest financial literacy organization in the country. And the key results indicate if we are achieving that.

One of our overall key results is that we are selling our material local, in the state, and across the country. We have an online version. We are ready to deploy new product. We have multiple clients in education. We're running workshops. Each one of those items is a KR, Key Result. Those are definitely measurable and quantitative. The goal is to look at OKRs on a regular basis.

If you were to search OKRs, you would find a bunch of different methods by which to use them. Yet, I like to make it very simple. Have an objective for the company, and then have a key results for that objective. After this, each department needs key results that align with the company's objective. This means those key results and their objectives are aligned with the company's objectives and key results. In turn, this means that each department is doing something very different that all funnels up towards obtaining an overall objective. It allows each department to be consistent.

If you can put an organization together like that, where you're all working together, it is dynamite. That's why we use OKRs.

Building Financial Language:

Define 3 KPIs and 3 KRs for a business. This can be a real or imagined company.

KPIs	KRs
1.	**1.**
2.	**2.**
3.	**3.**

9 Defining Company Culture

Watch video

https://youtu.be/YiWhOXBtk14

Does company culture go into a business plan? In my opinion, the answer is yes. I think company culture is so important, because it identifies exactly what kind of business you are.

I believe that culture equates to profitability.

It speaks to the quality of a business. In the end, this is something that's your decision. It's your choice. But if you want to have say about the kind of individuals you hire, the kind of goals and objectives you have for your employees must be clear.

As you bring more people into the business, and they each align with the culture of the company, the chances of them staying for a longer period of time (i.e. employee retention) is more likely because your company is more valuable.

Anybody that's working with you should want to make sure that you stay in business. The more valuable you are, the better it is for them as well. For employees to understand exactly what the company culture is, and to follow it, is therefore critical. To be able to convey that in a business plan, is important.

We can compare that to someone who invests in the stock market who also has a financial planner. If the financial planner is recommending certain investments in a particular fund, what is it that the investor is going to look for?

While yes, they will want to see the history of that fund, they are also going to want to look at the manager of the fund. Who is actually managing those funds? It does not matter if that entity is a person or is a company or a person in the company. We want to know that the holder of that information is someone we can trust We want them to be someone trustworthy who has a good track record.

> There are certain individuals
> that excel no matter what they do.

And if you knew who those people were, wouldn't you want them on your team? Those are the kind of people I want in my business. I want to make sure they are people I can relate with, that we resonate together and want to grow the business together. That way we are successful and every stakeholder is able to achieve their objectives.

Building Financial Language:

In your view, what makes a great company culture?

____

____

____

____

____

____

____

____

____

10 Steps To Create Your Business Plan

https://youtu.be/UF7kLXAhyNI

Watch video

Practically speaking, how do we create a business plan? Think about what we do when we get in the car and go to a new location. We get an address, take our phones, go into a map program, punch it in, and it gives us directions. Those directions are the plan. Of course, there's multiple steps within that.

But that's exactly what a business plan is.

It's a road map to achieving your objective. What's the first step? The first thing we need to do is make sure we know what our product is. Then we need to know who our audience is, who we're going to sell to, what the cost is, the selling price, and how we're going to distribute.

On your document, bullet point number one is the product and service. A paragraph or two below, write down what that all entails.

I recommended you speak to somebody who knows you and is familiar with your business idea. Ask them to write down what you do. We all know what we say, but do others hear it that way? Work with people you know. Ask them, "Would you do me a favor? Could you just write a description of what you think I'm selling?"

See if they can create a description of what you do, where you are going to sell it, and how it's going to be distributed. Are they able to recognize the main players? In the end, you basically have an outline of a business plan.

Remember, this does not have to be perfect.

It just has to have content. The content has to be real. And you have to be able to support it. You have need passion when you discuss it. You have to be excited about it. If you go to a bank and say: *Here's my business plan...* but you are not passionate about your product or service, they're not going to partner with you.

You've got to have energy. Be excited about putting your plan together because this is the first time that you have an opportunity to share exactly what you're going to do.

You're ready. You've been thinking about it. You've been writing things down. You've been taking notes. You've talked to a ton of people. Now is your day. This is the day that you're putting something together. Be proud of it. Until you're totally proud of it, keep redoing it until you are able to say, "This is a great product." Then you can go forward in complete confidence.

Building Financial Language:

Who have you been sharing your idea with? Ask them what you do and what your business has to offer. When can you next meet with them?

____

____

____

11 When To Yield

Watch video

https://youtu.be/TDvC6lVeASU

In Stephen Covey's book, *The Seven Habits of Highly Effective People*, he tells a story of a ship whose captain could see a light ahead. They recognized that if they stayed on course exactly as they were, they would end up having a direct hit where that light was.

Now, the light indicates that there's another ship in the area. So the captain signaled forward and communicated the issue. He pretty much commanded for them to change their course. The response came back, "No, we are not going to change our course, you change *your* course."

It went back and forth a few times, until they realized that what was ahead of them wasn't a ship. It was a lighthouse. If they didn't change course, they would head straight into the lighthouse. There was a total misinterpretation of what was happening. And it stemmed from one person's perspective, which was not right.

When you see a light, it is easy to assume it's another ship. But it wasn't another ship. *Why do I share this story*?

Because as you think about putting your business plan together, it might be easy to make certain assumption. But remember, the light may not be a ship.

It may be something else.

Don't assume that just because you haven't seen something before or you're not aware of it that that's what something is, that you know the solution.

Recognize too, that once the captain found out what it was, he had to take a big piece of humble pie in order to keep himself and his crew safe.

Humility is often part of business. But it is also part of our own growth and development. These are keys when we set out to establish a business plan. We have to be flexible.

Building Financial Language:

Have you ever had a light vs. lighthouse story? If so, share it here:

____

____

____

____

____

____

____

____

Your Take Action Challenge

Watch video

https://youtu.be/447Q9KvkVtM

Here is your call to action: I want you to create your own basic business plan. To start: Search online and look for a template or a model for your business plan. Find something that works for you.

We've already given you quite a bit of information. If you want to create your own outline, that's great. To start, build a very simple business model. You may only have to speak about one product and one type of audience and then create one budget outline.

Try to hit the key points.

Make sure you understand what has to be included in your plan in order to be able to present it to someone. And then take that plan and present it to somebody that you know is going to read it, that cares about you, and someone that you're willing to listen to. Then, be willing to listen to feedback.

When I do workshops and seminars, I want feedback. Our goal is always to make what we do better. It's painful. Don't get me wrong. I don't want to hear criticism or negativity. It's somewhat painful because we all have an ego, every one of us.

However, if I only hear, "Oh, it's great!" There's no improvement. Go to somebody who is willing to tell you the truth.

There's a book called *The Third Opinion*. It rallies around this idea that we all need somebody that just gives us a third opinion. Someone who has zero bias. That's what we need. We need somebody to come and tell us what they think.

Our challenge to you? Put something together that you could potentially present to someone who is bold enough to tell you the truth, but kind enough to do it with grace matched with great feedback.

Building Financial Language:

When in the next 1-2 weeks can you set aside 2-3 hours to put together, or improve on, your business plan?

____

____

____

____

____

Who can you reach out to who might be willing to give you a third opinion?

____

____

____

MONEY MATTERS UNIVERSITY
EQUIPPING YOU TO RETAIN WEALTH

Discussion #24

Financial Success

Discussion #24

Financial Success

Discussion #24

Financial Success

The Big Idea:

Defining your personal measure of success,
helps you to achieve it.

How To Define Financial Success

Watch video

https://youtu.be/EmlKPvg0rBU

Believe it or not, financial success is not necessarily equivalent to how much money we have in the bank. Financial success relates to the freedom we have in terms of believing we have enough to do the things we really need to do and want to do.

It goes back to the needs and wants conversation.

A need is focused on the minimum requirement. And if we can do the things we want to do, and enjoy our day-to-day, to me, that's financial success.

Financial success is less about a number, and more about an attitude. It's tied into our financial health within ourselves.

There are a number of people that grew up never feeling like they had financial success, because they were educated to never spend a dime over what they needed.

To me, that is very unfortunate. My parents were that way. And many of their choices created a lot of constraint when I was growing up.

My advice? Don't fall into traps like that. Be happy with what you have. As long as you can enjoy your day-to-day activities, and wake up every day with peace of mind with less stress and feeling comfortable—that's achieving financial success.

Building Financial Language:

What is your personal definition of financial success?

____

____

____

____

____

____

____

____

____

Indicators Of Financial Success

https://youtu.be/i9eBwNAKXW8

Watch video

What are some of the common indicators of financial success? Peace of mind. That's number one to me. I want to know that I can wake up every day knowing my bills are paid.

To me, that has been the most peace of mind I've ever had.

When I don't have to think about having to work more, or having to do things that I may not want to do, even if I'm doing something I love to do, I feel free. I find that the sense of *having to do something* to earn money creates anxiety.

I teach financial literary, and have been living with good financial principles for some time now, and even I can wake up at times with financial anxiety. It may not make any sense whatsoever, but every once in a while that happens.

So what do I do?

I take inventory of what I have all over again. I think about how grateful I am for what I've received and how I've been blessed to be able to provide for each incident in my life. When I look at it, I've always been able to put food on the table.

To me, that peace of mind is what an indicator of financial success looks like for me. Every day I wake up, I know that my bills are paid.

Many people have financial stress. They worry about whether or not they're going to make enough money, or they don't like their job, or they wish they could do something else.

To me, it's important to be able to love what you do and know that you're being rewarded properly for it. That is what I would advise you to pursue.

Building Financial Language:

What are three indicators you have which let you know you have reached a place of financial success?

What If I Can't Find Financial Success?

https://youtu.be/wEvU26nEp7Q

If you are asking the question, "What if I can't find financial success?" I want you to rephrase that to ask, why can't I *see* my financial success?

If you really believe you are not achieving financial success, the first thing I would ask is, "What is it that you're not achieving? What do you feel you need to achieve in order to have financial success?"

If there is not enough money to pay rent, that is a very serious issue. If it's more of: I can't afford to go buy a new car that's $100,000, then it takes us back to the question of need versus want.

If you are having trouble achieving financial success within your needs, it's important to reevaluate what's going on and why that is happening. More often than not, however, it tends to be a mindset of not achieving a standard of financial success because someone has been working their whole life and doesn't feel like they have much to show for it.

But they are not in a horrible financial position. They just do not have everything they want. Sometimes our objectives or our expectations are a little out of control. We have to adjust to those expectations.

And if you're in a situation where there's a need that you truly can't fill, there are programs that can assist you. There are government programs that can help you.

I would reach out to some friends and family. I've been in situations myself. I'm a cancer survivor. When I was going through treatments, many people asked to help financially, make meals, clean the house, and take care of projects that needed to be done.

Don't be afraid to say yes. When somebody asks to help you, don't be so prideful to say, "No, I don't need help, I can do it myself."

Sometimes we can't. I know I have needed help. And it was hard to say, "Yes, please help me." But that is part of living in community. I would encourage you to say yes.

Building Financial Language:

What obstacles, if any, stand in the way of you finding financial success?

4 Taking Stress Away From Money

Watch video

https://youtu.be/aJBfvtWFe5A

How do I reach a point in my life where money is not stressful? I wonder if the question is about money being stressful or more about the *lack* of money being stressful.

Is the need to earn money stressful? Or is a feeling of being stuck in a situation where you must earn money and feel as if you can't do something else the root of what causes you stress.

At the core of the question, we must break down where the stress is actually rooted.

What is the core issue? Is it a feeling of being at a certain age and there is concern you are not going to have enough to live on when you retire? Is it a feeling that you have never had extra. Is the stress sourced in feeling that needs are only met day-to-day, week-to-week, and paycheck-to-paycheck?

It's very important to identify where that stress is coming from. Because once we know the source, it may be easier to recognize we have more than we need. It just may not be what we want today.

Look at money as an incremental stress. Think of walking up the steps and asking yourself: Step one: Do I have enough for today? Next: Do I have enough for tomorrow? Looking further: Am I able to begin planning for next year? Further down: When I retire, will I be okay?

Sometimes the stress of money is less about having enough and more about an emotional attachment, or even competition.

I was with a financial planner the other day. The planner shared something with me, which I never really thought about. She told me, "Often individuals who inherit stock don't want to sell it, not because it's a good stock, but they don't want to sell it because it's a symbol of losing connection with their loved ones."

I never thought of it that way.

I don't think it is a good thing to hold onto something solely for an emotional attachment. Maybe you do. Yet, I imagine that the people we inherit from want to provide something meaningful. In holding onto it, it is not fulfilling the purpose it was intended for. While this is just one example, it is important to realize that emotional connections contribute to our financial stress. *My advice*? Find out what you need in a balanced way, and move through to financial peace, step-by-step.

Building Financial Language:

What factors contribute to any stress you feel regarding money?

____

____

____

How many, if any, are rooted in emotional connection?

____

____

5 Does Money Matter?

Watch video

https://youtu.be/cXepUrx-uR8

I was with a group of people the other night who were talking about how we need to teach children about money. It was very interesting to me. Somebody made the statement that most children they knew saw money as a bad word.

I didn't understand that. It opened my eyes to a different perspective. It made me realize that if money is constantly a topic of discussion and it creates stress and conflict, then money will be seen as a negative thing, something that causes a rift.

But money is not a bad word,
it is a tool to empower our goals.

When individuals ask what kind of business I am in, I like to say I am in the healthcare business. Because I really do believe this is a healthcare business. We're in the *financial* healthcare business. Because financial health is just as important as physical, mental, and spiritual health.

It's so important to make sure you're in a healthy environment, because it affects your mindset. When we talk about money matters, it is something that impacts our entire being.

The love of money, in my opinion, is not good. *Why*? Because I think if you just love money that you can get greedy. Before you know it, your entire life is all about money and acquiring more and more.

That's not what this is about.

We're talking about financial success. We're talking about being able to utilize what we have, not diminish our quality of life to acculmulate more than we need. Money does matter. It matters a lot.

Because without resources, we cannot survive. The question comes down defining to what extent it matters in *your* life.

You don't want money to control you.
You want to be able to control your money.

Building Financial Language:

How do you view the word "money?"

6 How To Define Your Personal Measure Of Success

https://youtu.be/rQJUvQ9NHT8

Watch video

I'd like you to define your personal vision of financial success. To do so, the first thing I want you to think about is what is really valuable to you. Your values drive what's valuable to you, what makes you tick, and gives you passion. These are the things which are valuable to you.

My advice? Those values are where you should focus your efforts for financial success. Having them present within your day-to-day gives you peace of mind and joy. In turn, it encourages you to continue doing more of what you love.

> I have heard it said: Do something you love
> and you'll never work for the rest of your life.

I believe that. But there is still a balance which is needed. If you overdo it, then you're going to end up hating it.

You never want to wear yourself out trying to get rich. However, you want to make sure that you align your efforts and goals towards doing things you love. And then, find a way to make a living out of it.

I love sports. When I think about how much a professional athlete makes to have fun, it amazes me. They're making money to play a game! Why don't we look at our tasks in the same way?

What we do is our game.

Maybe my game is sitting down and sharing a budget. I know it's going to sound crazy, but I've been in budget meetings where I say, "Okay, today is my Super Bowl." *Why*? Because that day is the day I shine. That is the day I'm get to let everybody know how they're able to achieve their goals. By providing them a plan and a budget, they have a way to achieve their goals. And that is important to me. I want to see people win.

To me, one of the most exciting days in my career is when I sit down with an individual who is absorbing the info and it gets them excited. I love watching them move to another level and realize there is a way for them to achieve their goals.

Building Financial Language:

What is your "Super Bowl?" How do you like to help others win, find joy, or discover solutions?

7 A Final Encouragement

https://youtu.be/Pw9ifEeqVZM

Watch video

As we have come to the end of our material, I want you to pause for a moment. Recognize that this is a beginning for you. You have an opportunity to take what you've learned and choose what's important to you.

You get to create the next stage of your life.

Hopefully you've been able to select your next action steps. If you have been able to find one or two or three things that resonate with you, we believe it can make a difference in your life.

It will only grow from there. Think of this moment as the start. Compare it to starting an exercise regimen. If you want to get into a better physical condition, or you're training for a marathon, there is a time in which to learn and then there is a time to train. After that, it is a beginning of a new lifestyle.

That's what this is all about. That's why we put this program together. This is the beginning. It really is.

The time we've spent together, we don't want to look at it only as a one-time event. It's been a process. It's something that never ends. It will continue. It's not the graduation of something. It's not a commencement, it's a continuation.

We want you, in every possible way, to be equipped to become the author of your own financial story.

And now, you get to write it.

Building Financial Language:

Now that we have completed our our time together, how do you see your financial legacy as just beginning?

Your Take Action Challenge

Watch video

https://youtu.be/447Q9KvkVtM

For this phase, I'm going to give you your final challenge. I'm going to ask you several questions. First, what did you hear? What resonated with you? And what is it that you really remember?

What do you not have to go back to any of your notes, or any of the videos, or any of the course, and it just comes right off your head? Take a moment to jot that down.

First: What have you heard?
Next: What are you gonna do about it?

Knowledge is power, but power only manifests itself in action.

It's your time to take action, to control your life. It's up to you, and we wish you the best success.

Building Financial Language:

As you have worked through this course, what did you hear? What resonated with you?

What learnings do you remember the most?

Next, what are you going to do about it? And when?

Glossary Of Terms

The Money Matters University Glossary of Terms is intended to be a resource for you, as you become the author of your financial story. The intention is to build your knowledge by providing our understanding of industry terms along with financial language our team has created in order to make finance simple. We are excited to partner with you and look forward to learning together.

401K Match: A 401(k) is an employer-sponsored retirement plan that allows employees to contribute a portion of their pre-tax earnings. Some employers match employee contributions up to a certain amount, thus increasing the compensation package for participating employees.[1]

ABC Players: "A" players are your top performers. They exceed the basic requirements of their job. They would be next in line for a promotion. - "B" players are your average performers. They meet the basic requirements of their job. They might be considered for a promotion. - "C" players are you lowest performers. They do not meet the basic requirements of their job. They would not be considered for a promotion.

Acquisition: The act of acquiring or gaining possession; the purchase of one business enterprise by another.[2]

Advance Payments: Sum that is paid or received in advance for goods or services.[3]

Adviser: A person with more and deeper knowledge in a specific area and usually also includes persons with cross-functional and multidisciplinary expertise.[4]

Alignment: The organization of activities or systems so that they match or fit well together.[5]

Assets: Any resource owned by a business or an economic entity, tangible or intangible, that could produce positive economic value.[6]

Balance Sheet: A tabular statement of both sides of a set of accounts in which the debit and credit balances add up as equal.A statement of the financial position of a business on a specified date·[7]

Bank Reconciliation: Summary of banking and business activity that reconciles an entity's bank account with its financial records.The statement outlines the deposits, withdrawals and other activities affecting a bank account for a specific period.[8]

Bank Statement: For each bank account held by a person or business with a financial institution.[9]

Benefits: Extra money or other advantages that you get in addition to your salary from your employer as part of your job.[10]

Bonuses: Something given or paid over and above what is due; something extra or additional given freely.[11]

Budget: An estimate, often itemized, of expected income and expense for a given period in the future. A plan of operations based on such an estimate.An itemized allotment of funds, time, etc., for a given period.[12]

Budget Philosophy: Overall approach and philosophy for budgeting and planning in Business and Finance, including common terminology, procedures, and principles used in that process. It is through this strategy that priorities can be ranked across Business and Finance to maximize available resources and provide the appropriate level of service for the costs incurred. It is only through a mutual understanding of strategic goals that a plan can be defined to accomplish them.[13]

Business goals: Business goals are goals that a business anticipates accomplishing in a set period.[14]

Capacity: Actual or potential ability to perform, yield, or withstand.[15]

Capital Expenditures: The money an organization or corporate entity spends to buy, maintain, or improve its fixed assets, such as buildings, vehicles, equipment, furniture or land.[16]

Cash Flow Model: A month by month projection of financial activity and cash balances.The primary purpose of the cash flow model is to establish visibility of cash balance to determine the ability to invest or the requirement for additional cash to effectively manage the business.

CFO: The chief financial officer(CFO) is officer of a company that has primary responsibility for managing the company's finances, including financial planning, management of financial risks, record-keeping, and financial reporting. In some sectors, the CFO is also responsible foranalysis of data. Some CFOs have the title CFOO for chief financial and operating officer. In the United Kingdom, the typical term for a CFO is finance director(FD). The CFO typically reports to the chief executive officer(CEO) and the board of directors and may additionally have a seat on the board. The CFO supervises the finance unit and is the chief financial spokesperson for the organization. The CFO directly assists thechief operating officer(COO) on all strategic and tactical matters relating to budget management, cost–benefit analysis, forecasting needs, and securing of new funding.[17]

Chart of Accounts: A chart of accounts (COA) is an index of all thefinancial accountsin thegeneral ledgerof a company. In short, it is an organizational tool that provides a digestible breakdown of all the financialtransactionsthat a company conducted during a specificaccounting period, broken down into subcategories.[18]

Clarity: The ability to be easily understood.[19]

Commissions: Variable-pay remuneration for services rendered or products sold.[20]

Compensation: Total cash and non-cash payments that you give to an employee in exchange for the work they do for your business.[21]

Continuing Education: Classes in which professional people learn the latest developments, laws, etc. relating to their professions.[22]

Cost of Goods (Sold): The direct costs of producing the goods sold by a company. This amount includes the cost of the materials and labor directly used to create the good. It excludes indirect expenses, such as distribution costs and sales force costs.[23]

Cost of Sales (COS): COGS include all costs of purchase, costs of conversion and other costs incurred in bringing the inventories to their present location and condition. Cost of goods made by the business include material, labor, and allocated overhead. The costs of goods not yet sold are referred as costs of inventory until the inventory is sold or written down in value.[24]

CPA: Certified Public Accountant,a State license to provide accounting and assurance services to the public.[25]

Culture: The set of shared attitudes, values, goals, and practices that characterizes an institution or organization.[26]

Culture (Training and Learning): In a training culture, responsibility for employee learning resides with instructors and training managers. In that kind of culture, the assumption is that trainers, under the direction of a chief learning officer (CLO), drive learning. In contrast, in a learning culture, responsibility for learning resides with employees, managers, and teams. In that kind of culture, employees are expected to seek knowledge and skills and apply that learning when and where it is needed.[27]

Days of Sales Outstanding: Days sales outstanding (DSO) is a measure of the average number of days that it takes a company to collect payment after a sale has been made. DSO is often determined on a monthly, quarterly or annual basis, and can be calculated by dividing the amount of accounts receivable during a given period by the total value of credit sales during the same period, and multiplying the result by the number of days in the period measured.[28]

Deferred Revenue: Money received for goods or services which has not yet been earned.

Delegate: The assignment of any responsibility or authority to another person.30

Deposits: Money placed in a bank account. Anything given as security or in part payment.[31]

Development: Growth, Progress and a significant consequence or event.[32]

Disaster Protection Plan: A set of instructions for how to respond to a major incident. The intent behind the plan is to bring the organization's operations back to full functionality as soon as possible.[33]

Discovery Sheet: A document established to assist our clients to identify their learnings related to their current business based on the midpoint of the MMU material.

Efficiency: The ability to work well and produce good results by using the available time, money, supplies, etc. in the most effective way.[34]

Employee: A person working for another person or a business firm for pay.[35]

Employee Roster: A list of employees and associated information for a given time period.[36]

Equity Options: Securities that give the holder the right (but not the obligation) to buy or sell a specified number of shares of stock, at a specified price for a certain (limited) time period.[37]

Escalation Process: An Escalation is a procedure that results from the pre-established set of parameters that moves a complaints, challenges, or concerns to either a more senior representative or one that initiates a related process.[38]

Executive Management Team: A team of individuals at the highest level of management of an organization who have the day-to-day tasks of managing that organization.[39]

Exit Interview: Survey conducted with an individual who is separating from an organization or relationship, the information gained from an exit interview can be used to assess what should be improved, changed, or remain intact.[40]

Financial (Funding) Institution: A financial institution (FI) is a company engaged in the business of dealing with financial and monetary transactions such as deposits, loans, investments, and currency exchange. Financial institutions encompass a broad range of business operations within the financial services sector including banks, trust companies, insurance companies, brokerage firms, and investment dealers. Virtually everyone living in a developed economy has an ongoing or at least periodic need for the services of financial institutions.[41]

Fixed Fee: A set amount paid for work or a service, that does not change with the time the work takes or the amount the service is used.[42]

Future cast: A patented, scientifically enabled platform that can help you gain greater insights into the mind and body, predict behavior, create richer interactions, and support the health of individuals and, at scale, entire populations.[43]

Glassdoor: A website where current and former employees anonymously review companies. Glassdoor also allows users to anonymously submit and view salaries as well as search and apply for jobs on its platform.[44]

Glossary: A list of terms in a special subject, field, or area of usage, with accompanying definitions such a list at the back of a book, explaining or defining difficult or unusual words and expressions used in the text.[45]

Gross profit: The profit a company makes after deducting the costs associated with making and selling its products, or the costs associated with providing its services. Gross profit will appear on a company's income statement and can be calculated by subtracting the cost of goods sold (COGS) from revenue (sales). These figures can be found on a company's income statement.[46]

Gross profit percentage: The margin earned (as a percentage) on a product or service after applying the total production cost to the revenue earned. The total costs include the cost of labor, materials, and overhead. The GPP helps to identify the profitability of the organization's products or services and is often time leveraged as a benchmark against competitors, or industry standards.[47]

Guard Rails: To ensure alignment with the organization's goals and objectives and to keep people on the right path.[48]

Historical (Traditional) budgeting: Traditional Budgeting is one of the methods used for the preparation of the budget by the company for the specific time period under consideration where the budget of the previous year is considered as the base using which budget of the current year is prepared i.e., current year budget is made by making changes in budget of last year.[49]

Holes - Red, Yellow & Green: Holes placed in the red category are not urgent. Their overall impact is low as it pertains to reaching your financial goals. A plan needs to be put in place for the hole to be filled within 3-6 months. - Holes placed in the yellow category are urgent but not critical. Their overall impact is medium as it pertains to reaching your financial goals. They need to be addressed within a 30-60-day period. - Holes placed in the green category are critical. They must be addressed. Their overall impact is high as it pertains to reaching your financial goals. They need to be addressed within a 30-day period.

Incentives: Something that makes you want to do something or to work harder, because you know that you will benefit by doing this.[50]

Income statement or Profit & Loss (P & L): An accounting of income and expenses that indicates a firm's net profit or loss over a certain period, usually one year.[51]

Independent Contractor: A person, business, or corporation that provides goods or services under a written contractor a verbal agreement. An independent Contractor does not work regularly for an employer but works as required.[52]

Insurance: A means of guaranteeing protection or safety.[53]

Insurance Policy: A contract between the insurer and the insured, known as the policyholder, which determines the claims which the insurer is legally required to pay.[54]

Intake Form: A document completed by our clients prior to learning the MMU material, to assist our team to customize the material according to their current needs.

Interview: A formal meeting in which one or more persons question, consult, or evaluate another person.[55]

Investment: The investing of money or capital in business, stock, etc. in order to gain profitable returns, as interest, income, or appreciation in value, using, or giving of time, talent, emotional energy.[56]

IRS/State Audit: A review/examination of an organization's or individual's accounts and financial information to ensure information is reported correctly according to the tax laws and to verify the reported amount of tax is correct.[57]

Job Description: A written narrative that describes the general tasks, or other related duties, and responsibilities of a position.[58]

Job Performance: The work related activities expected of an employee and how well those activities were executed.[59]

Job Title: A term that describes in a few words the position held by an employee.[60]

KPI's - Key Performance Indicators: The critical (key) indicators of progress toward an intended result. KPIs provide a focus for strategic and operational improvement, create an analytical basis for decision making and help focus attention on what matters most.[61]

Leader: A person who has commanding authority or influence.[62]

Leadership: The position or function of a leader, a person who guides directs a group.[63]

Legal Claims: C1) v. to make a demand for money, for property, or for enforcement of a right provided by law. 2) n. the making of a demand (assert a claim) for money due, for property, for damages or for enforcement of a right. If such a demand is not honored, it may result in a lawsuit. In order to enforce a right against a government agency (ranging for damages from a negligent bus driver to a shortage in payroll) a claim must be filed first. If rejected or ignored by the government, it is lawsuit time.[64]

Line of Credit: A preset borrowing limit that can be used at any time. The borrower can take money out as needed until the limit is reached, and as money is repaid, it can be borrowed again.[65]

Lines of Service (Business): Line of business(LOB) is a general term which refers to a product or a set of related products that serve a particular customer transaction or business need.[66]

Long-term: Covering a relatively long period of time:a long-term lease. Maturing over or after a relatively long period of time:a long-term loan; a long-term bond.[67]

Mentor: A wise and trusted counselor or teacher; an influential senior sponsor or supporter.[68]

Micromanage: To manage especially with excessive control or attention to details.[69]

Money Matters University: A 12-conversation education program that builds Financial Security, Strong Processes and Strong Organizations.

Morale: The mental and emotional condition (as of enthusiasm, confidence, or loyalty) of an individual or group with regard to the function or tasks at hand.[70]

Objectives: The manifestation of your VISION.

Org Chart: A diagram that shows the structure of an organization and the relationships and relative ranks of its positions/jobs.[71]

Organic Growth: Refers to the growth of a business through internal processes, relying on its own resources.[72]

Orientation Program: The general process of onboarding new employees and independent contractors conveying the organizations culture, understanding the org chart, and training according to their specific job responsibilities.

Ownership: Legal right of possession; proprietorship.[73]

Pain Point: A persistent or recurring problem (as with a product or service) that frequently inconveniences or annoys customers.[74]

Pitfalls: A hidden or not easily recognized danger or difficulty.[75]

Planning: An orderly or step-by-step conception or proposal for accomplishing an objective.[76]

Policy: A definite course or method of action to guide and determine present and future decisions.[77]

Procedures: A series of steps followed in a regular defined order.[78]

Processes: A continuous action, operation, or series of changes taking place in a definite manner.[79]

Products: A thing produced by labor:products of farm and factory; the product of his thought.[80] Also, the totality of goods or services that a company produces.[81]

Profit Margin: The difference between the cost of buying or making something and the price at which it is sold.[82]

Profit & Loss (P & L): An accounting of income and expenses that indicates a firm's net profit or loss over a certain period, usually one year.[83]

Promotion: An advancement in rank or position.[84]

Recruitment: The process of finding people to join a company or organization.[85]

Risk Management Assessment: Identifying and analyzing potential (future) events that may negatively impact individuals, assets, and/or the environment and making judgments "on the tolerability of the risk on the basis of a risk analysis" while considering influencing factors.[86]

Role: A function or position.[87]

Safeguard: Something that serves as a protection or defense or that ensures safety.[88]

Scalable: Capable of being easily expanded or upgraded on demand.[89]

Seagull Management: Manager-only interact with employees when there is a problem, they rarely offer praise or encouragement when things are going well. When problems arise, they often seek to place the blame on other people, and to draw attention to themselves in order to appear important. They criticize others, but make little contribution to the solution of a problem.[90]

Services: Commodities, such as banking, that are mainly intangible and usually consumed concurrently with their production.[91]

Short-Term: Occurring over or involving a relatively short period of time.[92]

SMART goals: SMART is an acronym that stands for Specific, Measurable, Achievable, Relevant and Time-based .Each element of the SMART framework works together to create a goal that is carefully planned, clear and trackable.[93]

Strategy: A plan, method, or series of maneuvers or stratagems for obtaining a specific goal or result:a strategy for getting ahead in the world.[94]

Subject Matter Experts: Asubject-matter expert(SME) is a person who is an authority in an area or topic.[95]

Subordinate: Subject to or under the authority of a superior.[96]

Succession Plan: Process for identifying and developing new leaders who can replace old leaders when they leave, retire, or die. Succession planning increases the availability of experienced and capable employees that are prepared to assume these roles as they become available.[97]

Supplier: Provide (a person, establishment, place, etc.) with what is lacking or requisite:to supply someone clothing; to supply a community with electricity.[98]

Sustainable: Capable of continuing for a long time at the same level.[99]

Take Ownership: An individual that receive authority and accept full responsibility to complete any task or project.

Tax Return: A report that a person or organization send to the government about the money that is earned and the taxes that are paid in one year.[100]

Teacher: A person who instructs or trains others.[101]

Time and Materials: Fee based upon the time spent to perform the work, and for materials used.

Titles: One or more words used before or after a person's name, in certain contexts. It may signify either an official position,a professional designationor academic qualification.[102]

Training: The process of learning the skills you need to do a particular job or activity.[103]

Training and Learning Culture: In a training culture, responsibility for employee learning resides with instructors and training managers. In that kind of culture, the assumption is that trainers, under the direction of a chief learning officer (CLO), drive learning. In contrast, in a learning culture, responsibility for learning resides with employees, managers, and teams. In that kind of culture, employees are expected to seek knowledge and skills and apply that learning when and where it is needed.

Values: To consider with respect to worth, excellence, usefulness, or importance.

to regard or esteem highly:He values her friendship.[105]

Values Assessment Questionnaire:A document developed to assess the current values of an organization.(See Values).

Vision: To see something in the future as it is today.

Zero Based Budgeting:A type of budgeting process where each expense item under consideration is evaluated from scratch for the new period and starts with zero and is taken only when its needs are fully justified.[106]

Glossary References

Unnumbered references, attributed to Richard Greco and Money Matters University © materials.

1. **401K Match:** https://www.thebalance.com/what-is-a-401-k-match-2894179

2. **Acquisition:** https://www.dictionary.com/browse/acquisition#

3. **Advance Payments:** https://en.wikipedia.org/wiki/Advance_payment

4. **Advisor:** https://en.wikipedia.org/wiki/Adviser

5. **Alignment:** https://www.macmillandictionary.com/us/dictionary/american/alignment

6. **Assets**: https://en.wikipedia.org/wiki/Asset

7. **Balance Sheet:** https://www.dictionary.com/browse/balance-sheet#

8. **Bank Reconciliation:**
https://www.investopedia.com/terms/b/bankreconciliation.asp#:~:text=A%20bank%20reconciliation%20statement%20is,account%20for%20a%20specific%20period.

9. **Bank Statement:** https://en.wikipedia.org/wiki/Bank_statement

10. **Benefits:**
https://www.macmillandictionary.com/us/dictionary/american/benefit_1?q=benefits

11. **Bonuses:** https://www.dictionary.com/browse/bonus?s=t

12. **Budget:** https://www.dictionary.com/browse/budget?s=t

13. **Budget Philosophy:** http://www.finance.umich.edu/analysis/budget

14. **Business goals:**
https://www.indeed.com/career-advice/career-development/business-goals

15. **Capacity:** https://www.dictionary.com/browse/capacity?s=t

16. **Capital Expenditures:** https://en.wikipedia.org/wiki/Capital_expenditure

17. CFO: https://en.wikipedia.org/wiki/Chief_financial_officer

18. Chart of Accounts: https://www.investopedia.com/terms/c/chart-accounts.asp

19. Clarity: https://www.macmillandictionary.com/us/dictionary/american/clarity

20. Commissions: https://en.wikipedia.org/wiki/Commission_(remuneration)

21. Compensation:

https://www.patriotsoftware.com/blog/payroll/what-is-compensation/

22. Continuing Education:

https://www.macmillandictionary.com/us/dictionary/american/continuing-education

23. Cost of Goods (Sold):

https://www.investopedia.com/terms/c/cogs.asp#:~:text=
What%20Is%20Cost%20of%20Goods,costs%20and%20sales%20force%20costs.

24. Cost of Sales (COS):

https://encyclopedia.thefreedictionary.com/cost+of+goods+sold

25. CPA: https://en.wikipedia.org/wiki/Certified_Public_Accountant
#:~:text=In%20the%20United%20States%2C%20the,to%20practice%20in%20their%20state.

26. Culture: https://www.merriam-webster.com/dictionary/culture

27. Culture (Training and Learning):

https://www.td.org/insights/from-a-training-culture-to-a-learning-culture

28. Days of Sales Outstanding: https://www.investopedia.com/terms/d/dso.asp

29. Deferred Revenue: https://en.wikipedia.org/wiki/Deferred_income

30. Delegate: https://en.wikipedia.org/wiki/Delegation_(disambiguation)

31. Deposits: https://www.dictionary.com/browse/deposit?s=ts

32. Development: https://www.dictionary.com/browse/developmental?s=t

33. Disaster Recovery Plan:

https://www.thebalancesmb.com/disaster-recovery-planning-goals-and-objectives-2533757

34. Efficiency: https://www.macmillandictionary.com/us/dictionary/american/efficiency

35. Employee: https://www.dictionary.com/browse/employee?s=t

36. Employee Roster: https://en.wikipedia.org/wiki/Roster

37. Equity Options:https://financial-dictionary.thefreedictionary.com/Equity+options

38. Escalation Process: https://www.taskus.com/glossary/escalation/

39. Executive Management Team:
https://en.wikipedia.org/wiki/Senior_management

40. Exit Interview: https://en.wikipedia.org/wiki/Exit_interview

41. Financial (Funding) Institution:
https://www.investopedia.com/terms/f/financialinstitution.asp

42. Fixed Fee:
https://www.ldoceonline.com/dictionary/fixed-fee#:~:text=From%20Longman%20Business%20Dictionary%20%CB%88fixed,for%20each%20medical%20service%20performed.

43. Future cast: https://www.pwc.com/us/en/products/future-cast.html

44. Glassdoor: https://en.wikipedia.org/wiki/Glassdoor

45. Glossary: https://www.dictionary.com/browse/glossary?s=t

46. Gross profit:
https://www.investopedia.com/terms/g/grossprofit.asp#:~:text=Gross%20profit%20is%20the%20profit,)%20from%20revenue%20(sales).

47. Gross profit percentage:
https://www.myaccountingcourse.com/accounting-dictionary/gross-profit-percentage#:~:text=Definition%3A%20Gross%20profit%20percentage%20is,labor%2C%20materials%2C%20and%20overhead.

48. Guard Rails:
https://tcagley.wordpress.com/2019/03/14/guardrails-in-decision-making/

49. Historical (Traditional) budgeting:
https://www.wallstreetmojo.com/traditional-budgeting/

50. Incentives: https://www.macmillandictionary.com/us/dictionary/american/incentive

51. Income statement or Profit & Loss (P & L):
https://www.dictionary.com/browse/income-statement?s=t

52. Independent Contractor:
https://en.wikipedia.org/wiki/Independent_contracting_in_the_United_States

53. Insurance: https://www.merriam-webster.com/dictionary/insurance

54. Insurance Policy: https://en.wikipedia.org/wiki/Insurance_policy

55. Interview: https://www.dictionary.com/browse/interview?s=t

56. Investment: https://www.dictionary.com/browse/investment?s=t

57. IRS/State Audit:
https://www.irs.gov/businesses/small-businesses-self-employed/irs-audits#:~:text=An%20IRS%20audit%20is%20a,amount%20of%20tax%20is%20correct.

58. Job Description: https://en.wikipedia.org/wiki/Job_description

59. Job Performance:
http://www.businessdictionary.com/definition/job-performance.html

60. Job Title: https://www.thebalancecareers.com/job-titles-a-z-list-2061557

61. KPI's – Key Performance Indicators: https://kpi.org/KPI-Basics

62. Leader: https://www.merriam-webster.com/dictionary/leader

63. Leadership: https://www.dictionary.com/browse/leadership?s=t

64. Legal Claims: https://legal-dictionary.thefreedictionary.com/claim

65. Line of Credit: https://www.investopedia.com/terms/l/lineofcredit.asp

66. Lines of Service (Business): https://en.wikipedia.org/wiki/Line_of_business

67. Long-term: https://www.dictionary.com/browse/longterm?s=t

68. Mentor: https://www.dictionary.com/browse/mentor?s=t

69. Micromanage: https://www.merriam-webster.com/dictionary/micromanage

70. Morale: https://www.merriam-webster.com/dictionary/morale

71. Org Chart: https://en.wikipedia.org/wiki/Organizational_chart

72. Organic Growth:

https://www.investopedia.com/terms/o/organicgrowth.asp#:~:text=Organic%20growth%20is%20the%20growth,through%20the%20company's%20own%20resources.

73. Ownership: https://www.thefreedictionary.com/ownership

74. Pain Point: https://www.merriam-webster.com/dictionary/pain%20point

75. Pitfalls: https://www.merriam-webster.com/dictionary/pitfall

76. Planning: https://www.thefreedictionary.com/planning

77. Policy: https://www.merriam-webster.com/dictionary/policy

78. Procedures: https://www.merriam-webster.com/dictionary/procedure

79. Processes: https://www.dictionary.com/browse/processes?s=ts

80. Products: https://www.dictionary.com/browse/product?s=ts & https://www.thefreedictionary.com/PRODUCTS

81. Profit Margin: https://www.merriam-webster.com/dictionary/profit%20margin

82. Profit & Loss (P & L): https://www.dictionary.com/browse/income-statement?s=t

83. Promotion: https://www.dictionary.com/browse/promotion?s=t

84. Recruitment:

https://www.macmillandictionary.com/us/dictionary/american/recruitment

85. Risk Management Assessment: https://en.wikipedia.org/wiki/Risk_assessment

86. Role: https://www.thefreedictionary.com/Roles

87. Safeguard: https://www.dictionary.com/browse/safeguard?s=t

88. Scalable: https://www.merriam-webster.com/dictionary/scalable

89. Seagull Management: https://en.wikipedia.org/wiki/Seagull_management)

90. Services: https://www.dictionary.com/browse/services?s=t

91. Short-Term: https://www.merriam-webster.com/dictionary/short-term

92. SMART goals: https://www.indeed.com/career-advice/career-development/smart-goals

93. Strategy: https://www.dictionary.com/browse/strategy?s=ts

94. Subject Matter Experts: https://en.wikipedia.org/wiki/Subject-matter_expert

95. Subordinate: https://www.dictionary.com/browse/subordinate?s=t

96. Succession Plan: https://en.wikipedia.org/wiki/Succession_planning

97. Supplier: https://www.dictionary.com/browse/supplier?s=t

98. Sustainable: https://www.macmillandictionary.com/us/dictionary/american/sustainable

99. Tax Return: https://www.merriam-webster.com/dictionary/tax%20return

100. Teacher: https://dictionary.cambridge.org/us/dictionary/english/teacher

101. Time and Materials: https://en.wikipedia.org/wiki/Time_and_materials

102. Titles: https://en.wikipedia.org/wiki/Title

103. Training: https://dictionary.cambridge.org/us/dictionary/english/training

104. Training and Learning Culture:

https://www.td.org/insights/from-a-training-culture-to-a-learning-culture

105. Values: https://www.dictionary.com/browse/values?s=t

106. Zero Based Budgeting: https://www.wallstreetmojo.com/zero-based-budgeting/

Made in United States
North Haven, CT
11 November 2026

22097461R00102